Eat Orgasmically

Eat Orgasmically and Still Lose Weight

Deanna Jepson, M.D. with Erica Brealey

Thorsons
An Imprint of HarperCollins*Publishers*

To my mother, a woman of vision

Thorsons
An Imprint of HarperCollins*Publishers*
77–85 Fulham Palace Road,
Hammersmith, London w6 8jb

First published by Thorsons 1997
This edition published by Thorsons 1999
1 3 5 7 9 10 8 6 4 2

© Deanna Jepson and Erica Brealey

Deanna Jepson and Erica Brealey assert the moral right to
be identified as the authors of this work

A catalogue record for this book
is available from the British Library

ISBN 0 7225 3834 0

Printed in Great Britain by
Creative Print and Design (Ebbw Vale), Wales

Contents

I thank my family, especially my husband Keith, my sons Duncan and Fergus, my brother Richard, and my friends all over the world for patiently listening to me incessantly talking about overweight problems and eating disorders.

A very special thankyou to my son Duncan, who has helped me uncomplainingly in more ways than one.

I am indebted to Frau Trude Steinbach of Vienna, a gourmet cook who taught me to eat orgasmically without guilt. Thank you to Patrick Budge whose love for fun and food kindled the concept of *eating orgasmically*.

I thank the committee and organizers of the British Association for the Study of Obesity and Disorders of Eating, Metabolism and Body Weight, and the European Association of Studies of Obesity for organizing congresses, lectures, and meetings which have helped me to expand my knowledge.

I would also like to thank Dr. Andrew Prentice, Ph.D. M.Rc, Dunn Clinical Nutrition Centre, Cambridge, and Professor John Blundell, Biological Psychological Department, University of Leeds, for their inspiring articles on obesity and eating disorders.

Finally, I thank the team at Thorsons for making this book possible.

Deanna Jepson, M.D.

As I began to write this book based on Dr. Jepson's system, I found myself thinking a lot about times I have been orgasmic over delicious confections such as Chocolate Nemesis from The River Cafe in London, or Sachertorte, the original version from the Hotel Sacher in Vienna. My digestive juices began to flow as freely as my creative juices and I started to eat orgasmically – rather too often. Naturally my weight crept up, until Deanna stepped in firmly and impressed upon me the art of compensation. My thanks to Deanna from saving me from a potentially fat fate, and for the fun we had during the writing of this book.

I would also like to thank all the staff at Thorsons, in particular: Christina Digby for her contributions to the script and her endless patience throughout the editing process, and Eileen Campbell for her kindness and thoughtfulness. I am also particularly grateful to Naomi Selig for the book's title, and to Becky Viney, Sarah Whitehead, and Deborah Walker for the many ways in which they helped. My special thanks also to Sue Buchanan, Alan Davey, and Vanessa Marsland for their support and sage advice.

My greatest debt and thanks are reserved for my husband Nick, for his support, advice, humor, and love – through thinness *and* fatness (mine, not his!). His love of good food and fine wines, and his ability to eat orgasmically, are legendary.

Erica Brealey

Introduction

Would you like to indulge your passion for the foods you love and still lose weight? Do you want to stay in shape without continuously dieting, denying your natural instinct for food, and depriving your taste buds? If so, eating orgasmically is tailor-made for you.

Eating orgasmically is a completely new approach to weight loss that works for *everyone*. It is a food-friendly system that allows you to eat whatever you like, whenever you like, in a normal, healthy and enjoyable way. The reason most overweight people find it difficult to lose weight and stay slim is that they have developed what I call a fat mind, a dieting mentality. This mindset tells them that the only way to lose weight is through depriving themselves of the foods they desire and need. Eating orgasmically changes all this and resets your mind. It is a dieter's dream come true. Once you have got into the rhythm of eating orgasmically you will find that you can not only eat what you like, but you can eat as much of it as you need to feel completely satiated and fulfilled. When you adopt this approach to eating you lose any excess weight and, because it changes your attitude to food and your eating behavior, you *keep* it off – without dieting. By employing the art of compensation and tuning into your food rhythms you will reduce your eating capacity, control your appetite, and wave goodbye to uncontrollable food cravings. You will be able to eat your favorite foods to your heart's content, *knowing how to stop*.

Eating orgasmically is based on over 25 years of observation, study, and the treatment of many thousands of patients including myself. It is the first medically proven system for permanent weight loss that really is diet free. This book has been requested by thousands of patients, and so, here it is.

The Truth about Dieting

Research has now officially proven what I have maintained for several decades – *that dieting doesn't work*. After more than half a century of dieting, diet gurus, slimming aids, and gimmicks of all descriptions, we're still getting fatter and fatter. At any one time seven out of ten women are dieting, yet since 1991 the average weight of British women has increased by 15 percent and that of men by 12 percent, according to Department of Health figures. Three out of four men and almost half the female population are overweight, while 13 percent of men and 16 percent of women are clinically obese. The same is true in much of Europe. The situation in America is worse.

Most people look and feel a lot better when they are slim. Personally, I hated it when I got fat. And however much we may be in favor of fat acceptance and against any form of discrimination, in particular "fattism," there are, and are likely to continue to be, social consequences to being fat. Fat people are less likely to get jobs in a competitive world or to further their careers, are less likely to be well-paid, and have lower self-esteem. Those who are obese—more than 20 percent over their ideal body weight—are less likely to be able to get health insurance because of the health risks associated with obesity. Obesity-linked conditions include coronary heart disease, strokes, hypertension, certain kinds of cancer, diabetes, arthritis, gall bladder disease, gout, and menstrual and ovulatory problems.

Most fat people want to lose weight—and for the past 50 years we have been led to believe that dieting is the only way to do it. The shelves in most bookshops groan under the weight of the sheer quantity of books devoted to diets of every description. But *whichever* diet you try, it is never the answer. However much weight you lose on a diet—and it can be dramatic—the chances that you will *stay* slim are, well…slim! A hefty 95 percent of people who diet put back all the weight they lose—and more. Dieting fails long term because inevitably, if you are on a low calorie or starvation diet all day or for several days, your blood sugar falls to a level where your body is screaming for food. When you diet you deprive your natural desire for food, and the more you diet and deny yourself the foods you love, the more obsessive you become about eating them. When you eventually eat, you go berserk and binge. Then you feel guilty and starve again, then binge again. Most dieters end up fatter than they were before they began trying to lose weight.

Dieting is not the solution to losing weight. It quickly becomes part of the problem as dieters inevitably develop an

3

unhealthy relationship with food through constantly curbing their appetites. Obsessive dieting is a form of eating disorder, an addiction which is bad for your body and bad for your mind. The health risks linked with rapid weight changes caused by yo-yo dieting are at least as serious as those associated with obesity, and the dieting mentality is one of guilt and oppression, of denying your natural instinct and passion for food. The patients I see at my clinics in the north of England discover that it is only when they stop dieting that they achieve permanent weight loss.

The Sweet Statistics of Success

Together with my colleagues I treat around 1500 overweight and obese patients each year—more than 18,000 patients in all since I opened my first clinic 20 years ago. Many of the people we see are seriously overweight or obese when they come for their first appointment, and many have a long history of dieting. Our patients are seen once a week by doctors and counselors who take their medical histories and their histories of weight gain. Together we unravel the reasons why they have gained weight, then their journey toward a permanently slim body begins.

Some overweight patients are offered a course of drug therapy under medical supervision to help them gain control and modify their eating behavior. In common with many other medical experts in obesity I believe that for some patients, drugs can be a very useful way to kickstart weight loss and retrain them into slim eating behavior. However, drug therapy should only be undertaken under the supervision of a qualified doctor with experience of treating weight problems and eating disorders, and only in conjunction with a weight-loss program involving cognitive therapy, designed to change the patient's attitude and modify their eating and drinking behavior. This enables patients to overcome the eating behavior that lies at the root of their weight problem and replace it with a way of eating and drinking suitable to their lifestyle, which, once established, can be continued without drug therapy. Without this, any weight lost inevitably piles back on the minute drugs are withdrawn.

Our clinics boast a 98 percent success rate with patients losing an average of 15–16 lb or 7 kg. Along with the pounds, they also shed their addiction to dieting. It is because of them, and for them, that I am writing this book. It is also for all of you—whatever your size—who want to be free from the oppression of the dieting mind to enjoy the foods you love while you get into or stay in shape. Anyone can regain and retain their correct shape using my simple and unique approach to slimming and staying slim.

Eat, Drink, and Be Merry

Eating and drinking should be satisfying and pleasurable at all times and, if you are a food lover as I am, at times you will want a really good blowout. When you are in the mood to eat, eating orgasmically encourages you to indulge yourself without guilt and devour the foods that titillate your taste buds to your heart's content, until you are completely satiated, relaxed and content. This is what I call experiencing a "food orgasm."

A little of what you fancy really does do you good—so long as you don't feel guilty about it. A healthy mind is just as important as a healthy body, and to achieve this *and* lose weight your desire for the foods you crave must be fulfilled. You really *can* eat as much as you want of whatever you want and still stay slim for life. When you deny yourself the foods you crave you feel unsatisfied, so you nibble or binge and you don't achieve permanent weight loss. I know this is true both from personal experience—I was once more than 40 lb overweight—and from over 30 years' experience of treating patients with weight problems and eating disorders.

It is the successes and occasional failures of my patients that have given me my greatest insights into the treatment of weight problems and eating disorders, but it was my own obsession with slimming and dieting that stimulated my medical interest and led me to devote most of my medical career to helping people to lose weight.

My Transformation

It started when my family and I arrived in England. We loved England, we loved the English, and we adored English food: rich milky chocolate, stodgy jam roly poly, sweets we had never ever seen in Singapore. We began to eat cooked breakfasts which were swiftly followed up with coffee breaks and cookies, two-course lunches, high tea with cakes and scones, then supper by the fire. It had never occurred to me that I could ever get fat—Chinese people are usually slim and petite—yet the mirror was beginning to tell me a different story. But it was only when I went to meet an old friend I'd not seen since before I left Singapore that the awful truth finally dawned. She didn't recognize me.

In my despair I ate more and more to comfort myself, while my wardrobe changed from containing stylish clothes that highlighted my previously petite frame to shapeless garments that shrouded my relentlessly expanding body.

One day a family friend, a general practitioner, handed me a diet sheet and my fat fate was sealed. All my favorite foods were forbidden. In my desperation to lose weight, I would begin each day with the zest of Jason in search of the golden fleece. With the strength of Samson I would avoid the "fattening" foods I loved, only to weaken by eating one of the sweet foods I craved. Once I tasted the forbidden fruit, I literally couldn't stop or control myself. As soon as the brakes were off I went careering downhill, fast. I would lose up to seven pounds in a few days then go on an enormous binge.

Realizing the diet wasn't working, I tried one diet after another. Being an obsessive personality, I was soon firmly entrenched on the dieting treadmill, and still fat. Was it my metabolism? Was I just destined to be fat? Depressed and neurotic about food, I alternately starved, then ate like a maniac. My weight yo-yoed wildly and I was filled with self-loathing for my lack of willpower, my inability to stick to a diet.

At the time I thought I was alone in my fat fate. Now I know better. Millions of men and women are trapped in an obsessive and dangerous cycle of yoyo dieting which can only be cured by a new attitude towards food.

Slim Behavior

It was my mother's comments which provided the solution to my problems. She thought all my talk of metabolism was nonsense. She said I just ate too much. She had noticed that her slender friends who never experienced any weight problems would eat whatever they fancied, but would stop eating once they were full and leave food on their plates. Her more corpulent friends would wipe their plates clean and come back for more. Although this may sound obvious, it highlighted the glaring fact that I had simply been eating too much.

I began to observe the eating behavior of naturally slim people. Slim people are not afraid of overeating, or "fattening" food, but when they have a very rich meal or overeat, they tend to compensate by skipping the next meal or eating very lightly. Look around you in any restaurant or gathering and you will see enviably slender people tucking into enormous meals with great gusto. You can be sure they will just have a piece of toast or fruit at the next meal. In contrast to dieters, who deny themselves the foods they love and eat little or nothing at mealtimes, but are unable to stop once they start eating, naturally slim people do not deprive themselves. Because they regularly experience food satisfaction, they remain in control of what they eat.

A Slim Body with a Fat Mind

Long after I had lost weight and regained my former shape, I still had what I now call a fat mind—the legacy of diets with their forbidden foods, special foods, combinations of foods and so on. I could feel my face becoming fatter whenever I ate "fattening" foods, especially the chocolate and sweet stodgy foods I adore. I had acquired a distorted body image and for years saw myself as much bigger than I really am. The power of the fat mind cannot be underestimated. Even famous beauties and sex symbols, for example Jane Fonda, have confessed to hating the bodies so admired and envied by the rest of us. A fat mind leads at best to misery and obsession, at worst to serious eating disorders such as anorexia and bulimia. This is why my weight loss system includes exercises to banish the fat mind and the dieting mentality forever.

My Philosophy of Eating

The simplest way to understand my philosophy of eating is to compare eating behavior with sexual behavior. A healthy attitude to sex is comparable with a healthy attitude to eating and drinking, whatever your sexual or food libido. My aim is to help all my patients and readers acquire a healthy, happy relationship with food. This is essential to losing weight and maintaining your ideal shape.

Passion for food is a wonderful gift of life. Food is orgasmic, not addictive.

Eat Orgasmically and Still Lose Weight

The cornerstone of my system is acquiring the *art of compensation*—that knack which slim people seem to have been born with. *Eating orgasmically* enables you to control how much and how often you eat. I believe, within the framework of a healthy and balanced diet which is essential for your body and mind, that *what* you eat is up to you.

In this book you will discover what your natural body type is and the approximate weight you should be. You will find out *why* you are overweight if you exceed this, and learn how your body works and what it needs. Equipped with this new information about yourself, you can tune into your food rhythms and tailor a way of eating and drinking to suit your lifestyle, while you watch the excess pounds slip away for good.

Eating orgasmically is a new way of thinking and a new way of looking at food and your relationship with it. It works for everyone, whatever your lifestyle and whether you are young or old, male or female, teenage, in your fertile years, menopausal, or on HRT. Using my unique system you will lose any excess weight and stay in shape for good, as I have done for over forty years.

EAT ORGASMICALLY ... AND ENJOY IT!

9

1

Food Orgasm: Eating and Sexuality

GOOD FOOD, LIKE GOOD SEX, is one of life's great pleasures. Luckily they are both good for us too—and indeed essential to our survival—so long as we do not abuse them by regular overindulgence or inappropriate usage. Much literature has been devoted to the aphrodisiac properties of certain foods, and the close links between food and sex, and between eating and sexuality, are universally acknowledged and reflected in all languages. We describe people we find sexually attractive as "tasty," "a dish," or even "delicious"; the names of sweet foods—"honey," "sweetie," or "sugarpie"—are used as terms of endearment; and the specifically female parts of the anatomy lend themselves to comparison with all sorts of luscious fruits and delectable foods. Just as fruits become ripe for plucking and eating, and good wines mature with age, so men and women become ripe for sex. As mature adults we have appetites not only for food, but for more carnal pleasures.

Our attitudes to sexuality often mirror our attitudes to eating. To many, the pleasures experienced during sex are comparable with those enjoyed at the dinner table and it is no coincidence that a delicious meal eaten in an intimate setting is often a prelude to seduction. For food lovers, eating and drinking are part of the foreplay. We get into the mood for eating and sex in similar ways—and one often leads to the other. Curiously, though, when it comes to losing weight, the close relationship between sex and food, and between sexual and eating behavior, has been completely overlooked.

The Taste Buds

The mouth, especially the lips and tongue, is not just the orifice through which food enters our bodies and through which all the sensations of food are transmitted. It is an erogenous zone, usually the first point of sexual contact. The tongue is the most sensual organ in the entire body. More than 9000 taste buds are embedded in the tongue and mouth of an adult, and in children they are even more numerous. Each taste bud contains elongated taste cells covered with *microvilli*, or minute sensory hairs, on their free surfaces. When we eat, these tiny hairs are stimulated and send messages to the brain through the nervous system, relaying the taste sensations generated by the food we are eating.

It is our taste buds which allow us to appreciate the different flavors and textures of food. Taste buds are highly promiscuous: variety titillates them and increases our appetite. We quickly become bored of eating just one sort of food. If, for example, you were to eat your favourite chocolate cake every day, your taste buds would become satiated. The cake would lose its novelty value and even its delicious taste. You can only eat so much of any one kind of food at a time. Even when you feel completely full up with a main meal and unable to eat another morsel, you will still find, amazingly, that you can somehow find room for chocolate mousse or sherry trifle, as though there were another stomach for pudding. Because of the lack of variety, diets which forbid certain foods or combinations of foods often result in a temporary weight loss. But they torture our taste buds, frustrate our food instincts, and are nutritionally unsound. When we follow our instincts and satisfy our taste buds, our natural desire for variety ensures that we receive all the nourishment we need.

Another feature of our taste buds is their adaptability. The more you drink of a very sweet drink, the less sweet it tastes; the more you accustom your taste buds to sugar, the more sugar they crave. The reverse is also true. You may enjoy tea with sugar but if you were to stop putting sugar in your tea for a couple of months, then try it with again, you would find it unbearably sweet because your taste buds would have become accustomed to it without.

By understanding and making friends with your taste buds— neither depriving them of the variety and tastes they crave, nor overwhelming them with choice, and by manipulating their adaptability, you can learn to control your appetite and reduce, or modify, your eating and drinking capacity. This way you can enjoy your food while you lose any excess weight and stay in shape forever.

Food Satisfaction

Whether you consider yourself a food lover or not, enjoying your food and feeling satisfied after eating is natural, normal, and, I believe, essential to achieving and maintaining weight loss. Food satisfaction is a complex combination of sensations which everyone experiences in different ways according to individual tastes. But just as a baby needs regular feeding every few hours with human or formula milk—we would never even dream of restricting a baby's intake or giving it only skimmed milk—and will cry incessantly when it feels hungry, to be satisfied we all need to eat sufficient "filler" foods, foods of the right texture and density to fill our body's capacity for food, two or three times a day.

Simply stoking up with filling foods such as pasta, rice, bread, or baked potatoes satisfies our physical sensation of hunger, but not necessarily our appetite, our *desire* for food. Unlike a baby, who just needs a full stomach to feel content, we have appetites for food which have nothing whatever to do with hunger. Our minds as well as our bodies crave satisfaction from the food we eat, and what stops us from eating more is not just a full stomach, but the satisfaction of having enjoyed what we have eaten, and of having eaten what we wanted. When you feel full after a meal that you have enjoyed, your taste buds and stomach relax. Food satisfaction is like a plateau—level, balanced, steady. When your mind and body are in this satisfied, stable condition, you are in complete control of what you eat.

Self-control, not willpower, as I will explain later in the book, is the key to enjoying your food and eating orgasmically. Being the master of what you eat, rather than the slave, is essential to maintaining a happy, healthy relationship with food. To achieve this you need to eat enough to feel satisfied and to enjoy it.

Food Orgasm

If food satisfaction is a plateau, food orgasm is a peak. Not everyone can experience food orgasm just as not everyone can experience a sexual orgasm, but if you really love your food, you will know what I mean.

Your taste buds are highly sensitive. The thought, sight, and especially the smell of appetizing food excites your taste buds just as lustful thoughts or the presence or smell of someone you find physically attractive stimulates your desire for sex. Like our desire for sexual fulfillment, we also long to experience the climax of consumption. Once you are sexually aroused, you need to satisfy your desire; so, when you're in the mood to eat and your mouth is watering in anticipation of food, you need to eat enough of the foods you want, desire or crave, to peak. When tasting the foods you crave stimulates you to eat more and more until you have totally exhausted your taste buds, leaving them completely satiated and relaxed, then you have experienced food orgasm.

Just as each individual's experience of sexual orgasm is unique, and varies from one occasion to another, the experience of food orgasm is different for everyone. Peak food experiences can be triggered by chocolate truffles, candy bars, or pastrami sandwiches, depending on your own food passions. If you are a chocolate lover as I am, then the moment you even think of chocolate your heartbeat quickens, adrenaline flows, and you begin to salivate. Once you taste it you are stimulated beyond control and, if you have a highly developed food libido like mine, you won't be satisfied until you have got at least four, five or even six Peppermint Patties or Mars bars inside you. Of course a more refined taste with a lower libido might peak with just one or two delicious hand-made chocolates, slowly savoring the exquisite explosion of their taste buds. And just as the thrills of quickie sex can be as intense and erotic as a more leisurely encounter, sometimes a swift melt-in-the-mouth chocolate gulped down on the run can really do the trick.

When you go "mmmm" as you taste the food you adore, when nothing else matters except the enjoyment of food, when you feel completely replete and need nothing more, you are experiencing food orgasm.

Just as some people achieve multiple orgasms, really intense eating experiences can be multiorgasmic. Generally, though, if you have good sex you don't need it throughout all your waking hours and the same goes for orgasmic food experiences (in contrast to food satisfaction, which you need to experience at least once or twice a day). To begin with, if you are overweight, have a history of dieting or eating disorders, and especially if you have a highly developed food libido, it

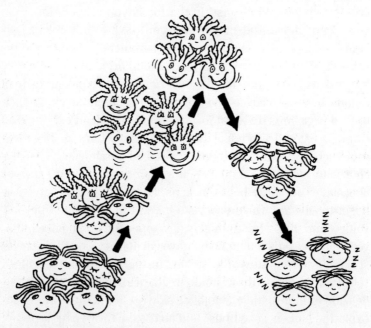

Taste buds before, during, and after food orgasm

is best to go for peak food experiences once or twice a week while you lose weight and/or retrain your eating habits. Once you have acquired the art of eating orgasmically so that it has become second nature and you are fully in control, the sky is the limit. Feast on whatever you fancy, peak as much and as often as you want, and *enjoy it*!

What Happens When You Fail to Achieve Food Satisfaction?

Our attitudes to food often reflect our attitudes to sex. Healthy adults derive great pleasure and enjoyment from the satisfaction of their desire for both food and sex. Lack of satisfaction in either department lies at the heart of many eating disorders and weight problems.

When you deprive yourself of the pleasure and satisfaction of eating well, when you deny yourself your favorite foods for the sake of losing weight, you inevitably fail. Most dieters try to exist on amounts of food they would never dream of imposing on their children or partners: a serving spoon of muesli for breakfast with just enough low-fat milk to moisten it, a tiny salad for lunch. They start to believe that food—or at any rate some kinds of foods—is bad for them. They virtually starve all day and then wonder why their willpower is so weak when, denied both the quantity and quality of food they need to satisfy body and mind, they lose control and resort to nibbling or bingeing. In fact, on a diet of deprivation, nibbling, and even bingeing, are in some ways normal responses—the body's way of telling you to change the way you are eating, that you are not getting the nourishment and satisfaction that you need. If you carry on ignoring the body's message to eat properly, you get caught in the trap of dieting, you spiral out of control, and develop a guilty, obsessive relationship with food.

Nibbling

When you pick, nibble, graze, or snack, nine times out of ten it is because your body is not getting what it needs and you are unsatisfied. Unsatisfied with the kind of food you are getting, unsatisfied with the amount you are getting or, most often, unsatisfied with both. True, some people—usually slim ones—nibble because they just happen to want to, and they nibble without being oppressed by or guilty about what they eat. But when fat people nibble, it is nearly always because they are not satisfied.

What happens in sex if you do not peak? Or if you are not sexually satisfied with your partner? You feel frustrated and dissatisfied and you may start looking around you for someone else. Likewise, if what you really want is three bars of chocolate and you get a few lettuce leaves dressed with oil-free

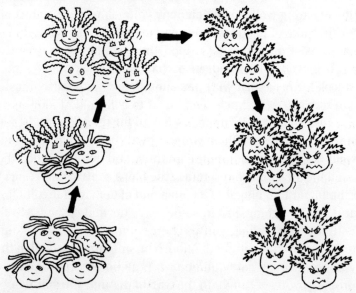

Nibbling leads to frustrated taste buds

vinaigrette, far from being satisfied, your appetite is simply whetted, your taste buds stimulated, and you are likely to start looking for something a little more tempting.

This is what happens when you are forbidden particular kinds of foods—usually your favorites—or particular combinations of foods, or when you force yourself to eat unappetizing "slimming" foods. If, like my husband, your idea of heaven on a plate is a generous serving of succulent roast lamb with crisp, crunchy oven-roasted potatoes and parsnips, washed down with a good claret, then you are about as likely to feel satisfied with a slice of boiled mutton, a helping of "dry" roasted potatoes and parsnips, and a Diet Coke, as you are to enjoy sex and reach orgasm with a robot. You cannot be satisfied sexually with a partner who is not sexually appealing to you, and you cannot achieve food satisfaction with food you find unappealing. When you are constantly eating low-calorie, low-fat, low-fun diet foods, your taste buds are continuously aroused and never satisfied. Eventually you lose control and begin to nibble at anything and everything in the vain attempt to satisfy your increasing appetite. Nibbling tickles the taste buds and gets you in the mood to eat. If you eat enough of the filler foods your body needs and enough of the appetizing foods you desire, you will be able to control your eating and drinking. But if they remain unsatisfied, the taste buds become irritated. When dieters nibble, they usually get into the mood to eat all the time and cannot stop. Once they start nibbling, dieters often end up on a binge.

Bingeing

A binge is an inhibited food orgasm. You binge when you use your will to abstain from eating the foods that you love, or from eating at all. You go for as long as you can, eating as little as you can, until you snap out of control. Because you have deprived yourself of the food you really need, want, or desire, you go mad and overeat on anything and everything. All dieters are a bit obsessive: one "wrong" food and you have spoiled the entire day, so you may as well stuff yourself till you can eat no more and start afresh with a clean slate tomorrow. You cram as much food as you can into your mouth, frantically stuffing it all in and wolfing it down as fast as you can. You can eat an entire packet of cookies in just a few minutes on a binge. But because you did not really want all the food you are cramming into your mouth, and because you are probably eating the food that first came to hand rather than the food you really crave, you do not enjoy it. You feel guilty afterwards and wish you had not eaten.

The sexual counterpart to bingeing is exemplified by making passionate love, then wishing you had not done it and feeling guilty and remorseful. This is a typical reaction of people who have been indoctrinated with the belief that sex is wrong, or sacred to marriage for the sole purpose of procreation. But if you have a passionate nature and a high libido, however much you try to deny or inhibit them, sooner or later—and it is usually sooner—they will find an outlet for expression. If you constantly deny yourself sexual satisfaction, you may end up sacrificing the potential for a good sexual relationship for sexual overindulgence with few peaks and a lot of guilt, and ultimately unable to enjoy sex at all.

Likewise, if you deny yourself food satisfaction, you can end up on a bender lasting days or all week because your taste buds are so aroused that your first thought when you wake in the morning is food. When you binge habitually, you sacrifice the pleasure of a happy relationship with food for a cycle of starving and bingeing, guilt, and obsession. It is but a short step from bingeing to food phobia and serious eating disorders.

Food Phobia

Wallis Simpson, the Duchess of Windsor, famously remarked that a woman can neither be too rich nor too thin. A sufferer from food phobia—she just picked and played with her food—she encapsulated with this comment the attitude of all women with food phobia and other eating problems.

Food phobia or food fear develops when you become so obsessed with dieting that it begins to rule your life and everything centers around your weight and what you eat—or do not eat. "Forbidden" foods—indulgent foods or anything with a high fat, carbohydrate, or sugar content—are eliminated as food phobics use iron willpower to abstain from eating the food they crave. Frightened that if they eat normally they will lose control, they inhibit their desire and rigidly maintain a strict diet. If they find themselves in social situations involving food, they just toy with their food, playing with it but hardly eating it. They refuse puddings, declaring that they dislike them when in reality they love them.

Food phobics never feel thin enough, even when they have stopped eating all the foods they love. They develop a distorted body image, seeing themselves as much fatter than they really are. Deprived of any stimulation, their taste buds are ruthlessly suppressed as they force themselves to eat only low-calorie and "healthy" foods, and replacement meals that they dislike, and eventually come to hate. They may also become keep fit fanatics, exercising stringently to keep their minds off food. Eventually their taste buds are completely annihilated. Obsessed with dieting to the point of food frigidity, they are prone to anorexia nervosa and bulimia nervosa, serious eating disorders which are becoming increasingly common both amongst men and women as they lose their sensuality, their lust for food and life, and finally their sexuality.

Anorexia Nervosa

The overwhelming preoccupation of anorexia sufferers, mostly women in their teens, is their relentless desire to be thin, even to the point of emaciation. Ruled by their obsessive fear of food and of gaining weight, anorexics resort to a variety of means in order to control their weight. Most drastically reduce the amount of all kinds of foods, especially "fattening" foods, and often exercise strenuously while they avoid food as far as possible in their quest to become ever thinner. Some anorexics—about 40 per cent—binge, then employ the "damage limitation" techniques used by bulimics: vomiting or using excessive quantities of laxatives and diuretics.

Even though anorexics are underweight, sometimes severely so, their own perceptions of their bodies are so grossly distorted that they feel fat even when emaciated. Women with anorexia stop menstruating, and other symptoms include hypersensitivity to hot and cold temperatures, a growth of soft downy hair on the face, back and arms, slowing down of the heart rate, low blood pressure, severe mineral and vitamin deficiencies, osteoporosis, broken sleep, and mental disturbances. Some anorexia sufferers literally starve themselves to death.

Anorexics are frightened of food. They are often shy about sexuality, and if they do form a long-term relationship, their happiness often depends on whether or not they feel secure and loved by their partner. Audrey Hepburn, the personification of glamor and beauty in the eyes of millions, nevertheless had a distorted body image, was insecure about her looks, and unconfident sexually. A recent biography has revealed that she suffered a turbulent love life punctuated by bouts of anorexia.

Anorexics are also found amongst the sexually passive, who may become involved in sexual relationships, but generally only when they are neither over- nor underweight. They tend to be unresponsive even then, and do not admit to enjoying sex. Like the sexually unsure, they often use their eating disorder to avoid sexual commitment, for example by choosing partners who are unavailable for long-term commitment. They prefer cuddling up with their partners and being held, and may accept sex as a means to this end.

Many anorexics go on to develop bulimia, which is more common than anorexia, and increasingly so, amongst both sexes.

Bulimia

Obsessive dieting in food lovers who use their willpower to suppress their love of food leads inevitably to compulsive bingeing; and bingeing can lead to self-induced vomiting, one of the classic symptoms of bulimia, as dieters purge themselves of the food they have just eaten rather than allow it to settle on their hips. Often linked with celebrities, such as Jane Fonda and Princess Diana, bulimia involves frequent bingeing sessions— at least a couple of times a week—strict dieting or fasting in between, often combined with obsessive exercise, and regular purges either by vomiting or by abusing laxatives, or both.

Bulimia shares many features with anorexia, but most bulimics are generally within the normal weight range or slightly overweight. Like anorexics, they are unhappy with their shape and weight; unlike anorexics who are underweight and often emaciated, they can remain in shape, yoyo wildly, or be out of shape. Typically in their teens or early 20s when they begin compulsive eating, bulimics have a love–hate relationship with food – they think about food much of the time and are often good cooks, but are afraid of the "fattening" effects of food. They diet strictly because they want to be slim and are frightened of putting on weight but,

23

because they still like food, when their willpower cracks and they eat something "forbidden," they cannot stop. They devour anything and everything in sight. After the binge they feel fat and bloated and ridden with guilt. Hating themselves for their lack of willpower, vowing never to binge again, they vomit on purpose, ridding their bodies of all the unwanted food, "raping" their taste buds in the process, and losing their self-esteem.

Frequent self-induced vomiting over a period of time rots the teeth, as the acid vomit eats away at the tooth enamel, and causes puffiness of the face owing to swollen salivary glands. More seriously it can result in dehydration, disturbances to the electrolytes in the blood, irregular heartbeats, and kidney problems. Laxative abuse can lead, amongst other things, to potassium deficiency and stomach cramps.

Bulimia is associated mainly with sexually assertive men and women, who mirror their eating behavior—a cycle of strict dieting, bingeing, and purging—with their sexual behavior. When they are up they are on the top of the world, the life and soul of the party. But although they tend to be socially active, this can hide an underlying feeling of loneliness and they often find it difficult to form long-term relationships.

Bulimia is also found amongst the sexually passive (*see Anorexia Nervosa, page 22*). Sexually passive types may be born that way, but often they are fundamentally passionate people who have become passive through dieting. Most bulimics can only become sexually stimulated when they feel thin.

If they never feel thin enough, bulimics may diet and purge more and more until eventually they lose their sexual and food libidos altogether. Once they reach this stage, they develop anorexia nervosa.

Recovery

Most people with eating disorders—food phobia, anorexia, bulimia, or more atypical ones—can and do recover, although severe cases of anorexia may occasionally warrant hospitalization. Over the years in my clinics I have watched in wonder as sufferers of anorexia and bulimia, as well as the overweight and obese, transform themselves from obsessive dieters and foodaholics to having a healthy relationship with food. Losing their fear of food and learning the art of eating, they have not only begun to enjoy their food again, sometimes for the first time in many years, but they are in perfect shape.

Are You a Food Lover?

Are you passionate about food or frightened of it? Do you eat what you like and enjoy it, or do you feel guilty when you succumb to temptation and eat "forbidden" food? Do you keep slim naturally or are you a professional dieter? Eating should be pleasurable and satisfying, not a source of inner conflict and tension. Recognizing and understanding your feelings and attitudes towards food is the first step on the way to eating healthily and happily if you are not already doing so. Test your food libido with the following quiz and find out how sensual your taste buds are and how you relate to food. Choose the option that best describes you, your eating behavior, and the way you think and feel about food.

Test Your Food Libido

1. *How often do you think about food?*
(a) Mainly when you are hungry, shopping for and preparing food, and at mealtimes.
(b) Quite often, especially when bored, slightly stressed, or emotionally upset.
(c) Most of the time.

2. *When you shop for food do you generally buy:*
(a) a balanced mix of basic foods and foods you especially enjoy?
(b) the basics, and anything else that takes your fancy (often in industrial quantities)?
(c) low-fat, low-calorie, "lite" or diet foods and drinks?

3. *Do you keep nibbles in the house:*
(a) mainly when entertaining or for special occasions?
(b) always—life would not be worth living without your favourite snacks?
(c) rarely—but when you do you overbuy and overeat?

4. *You are out to lunch or dinner, and after the main course you are offered a highly orgasmic dessert. Do you:*
(a) accept with pleasure and enjoy every mouthful?
(b) eat what you are offered with great gusto and come back for more?
(c) refuse, or eat as little as you can politely get away with, even though you are salivating at the mere sight of it?

5. *After a good meal out, are you likely to feel:*
(a) full and well satisfied, having eaten orgasmically?
(b) like eating more—your taste buds have just got going?
(c) fat, bloated, and guilty?

6. *Do you normally:*
(a) eat regular meals with only the very occasional nibble?
(b) eat whatever you fancy, whenever you fancy?
(c) diet, starve, or nibble all day, and eat—or overeat—in the evening?

7. *When cooking or preparing everyday meals do you:*
(a) prepare enough for normal servings all round?
(b) overcook—you do not want anyone to go hungry?
(c) avoid "fattening" or "forbidden" foods, at any rate for yourself?

8. *How does severe anxiety and stress affect your appetite and your weight?*
(a) You lose your appetite and you lose weight.
(b) You turn to food for relief and gain weight.
(c) You eat more erratically than ever, and may start bingeing and purging if you are not already doing so.

9. *Would you describe your sexual libido as:*
(a) normal to high?
(b) high?
(c) low?

10. *Do you feel:*
(a) relaxed about your body and what you eat (although you might like to lose a bit of weight)?
(b) overweight and often out of control; even if you diet, it does not last for long—and neither does the weight lost?
(c) preoccupied with your size and shape; you are constantly dieting?

If You Scored

You have a healthy and relaxed attitude to food and enjoy the satisfaction of eating well without being food mad. You do not think of foods as being "bad" or "forbidden," and though you generally eat a sensible and well-balanced diet, you have no qualms about indulging yourself if you feel like it and eating orgasmically. When you do, your taste buds may be satiated by a small bar of the best chocolate, or it may take a huge plateful of chilli con carne to satisfy you. Your food libido, like your sexual libido, is probably normal to high. If high, then you have learned to control your taste buds and, consciously or unconsciously, you are practicing the art of compensation.

You are usually in shape, your weight fluctuating gently, but you may become slightly apple- or pear-shaped if you overeat without compensating. If you are putting on weight it is probably because you have changed your lifestyle, or you have a new partner who enjoys his or her food, and you have started to eat more without really realizing. In the unlikely event that you are completely out of shape, it is most likely because you have been conditioned from childhood to overeat.

Even if you diet, you are not prone to becoming obsessive about it, although if for any reason you dieted strictly you too might develop the dieting mentality and see your weight begin to yoyo. Whatever your shape, you will lose and keep off any excess weight easily when you get into rhythm and start compensating.

MOSTLY (B)S
You have a very high food libido. You adore food, and may even be obsessive about it. You certainly know how to eat orgasmically but you tend to overdo it! Your taste buds are

28

easily aroused and extremely sensual, and once you start eating foods which excite your taste buds, you find it impossible to stop. You eat orgasmically—and would like to do so all the time. You turn to food both to reward yourself and for comfort: if you have been promoted, you celebrate with the most fabulous meal or the most orgasmic death-by-chocolate cake that you can obtain. If you are stressed, depressed, or stuck at home and bored, you raid the refrigerator and the kitchen cabinet.

You are more often out of shape than in shape. Your taste buds are constantly being titillated, with the result that you gain weight and increase your eating capacity. If you diet you are very likely to acquire the dieting mentality—you have an obsessive personality—and your weight will yoyo, often quite dramatically. You probably have a very high sex drive, and can be a terrific lover when you look and feel good. However, when your weight goes above a certain level you feel unsexy and your libido is dampened.

Because you live to eat, you need to eat orgasmically at least once a week, and should never ban any foods from your diet—you will become even more obsessed with them if you do, and eventually you will binge. Mastering the twin arts of eating and compensating will modify your eating behavior. Get into rhythm as soon as you can—the quiet rhythm will calm down your excitable taste buds. You will be amazed how easy it is to eat orgasmically and lose weight!

MOSTLY (C)S

You are a professional dieter, probably with a high food libido, but your taste buds are being suppressed and depressed by dieting foods, and you have lost the art of eating orgasmically. From being a passionate food lover, you have developed a tense love–hate relationship with food because obsession with your weight has resulted in obsession with it. Your strong willpower enables you to abstain from "forbidden" foods for days and even weeks at a time, but the more you deprive your-self, the more you cannot stop thinking about food. When you give in to temptation and eat "banned" foods, you often lose control and binge. Unfortunately you rarely enjoy your binges because you feel guilty about eating, and bad about yourself for what you mistakenly see as your lack of willpower.

You may be slim, or you may suffer from the yoyo weight syndrome. Although you appear to be highly in control of yourself and what you eat, in reality you have a fat mind (*see page 8*) and are liable to food phobia and other eating disorders if you continue to diet and/or exercise obsessively. Your naturally normal or high sexual libido is probably inhibited along with your taste buds, so it may appear low.

If you have picked up and are reading this book then deep down you probably already know that dieting is not the answer either to getting or staying in shape. The three mental exercises described in Chapter 5 will help you to overcome your fat mind—your fear of food and the guilt that goes with it. Get into rhythm, reduce variety for the first week or two, but be sure to eat orgasmically once or twice a week, allowing your taste buds to flower and peak again.

MOSTLY (A)S AND (B)S

Like the (a) group, you have a pretty relaxed attitude to food, and you certainly enjoy eating. Like the (b)s, you have a high food libido and you are prone to putting on weight from time to time, especially if you have an active social life involving a lot of eating, and also when you are going through difficult times.

You need to tune into your own rhythm as soon as you can and practice the art of compensation consciously, and discover the orgasmic way to deal with the munchies when you get them!

MOSTLY (B)S AND (C)S

You have a very high food libido and enjoy your food tremendously, but you hate being out of shape so you keep an eye on your weight. Because you let go and eat with abandon on occasion – at Christmas, on holiday, or with a new lover – and you also reward or comfort yourself with food, your weight can shoot up by seven pounds before you know it. You then diet, but it does not usually last long. When you cut down and avoid the foods you love, your desire for them becomes overpowering and the diet gets broken.

If you continue to diet, you will certainly develop the dieting mentality. Tune into your food rhythm now and start practicing the three mental exercises in Chapter 5 before any real damage is done. Using the art of compensation you will find you can enjoy the food you love so much, yet still lose weight.

MOSTLY (A)S AND (C)S

You also have a high food libido, but combined with a fairly healthy attitude to food and very strong willpower, so you are unlikely to be seriously out of shape. You rarely have more than 7 lb to lose. Although you really love your food, and will eat orgasmically when you go out, you are always dieting— even though it never seems to work!

End your obsession with dieting and start eating orgasmically now to lose any excess weight and stay in shape permanently. If you have only seven pounds or less to lose and are not in a hurry, you can go straight into the control rhythm described in Chapter 9.

2

Dietmania: The Fast Road to Fat Profits, Fat Bodies, Fat Minds

Dieting is a national epidemic. At any moment in time at least one in four of us—and more than half of the female population —is on a diet. Thinness is idealized and glamorized. Fashion magazines and advertisements create dreams and fantasies for us to aspire to, featuring an endless stream of long, leggy, ravishing size 6 models. It is no wonder that the average woman, at size 12, feels undermined and inadequate, desperate to lose weight and change shape to conform with the fashion and beauty ideals of the moment, and so is a prime target for the slimming industry with its myriad diets, pills, and potions.

Fat Profits

Dieting is big business. Driven by potentially huge profits and massive marketing, fueled by the media, and preying on our insecurities and obsessive desire to be thin, the slimming industry in Britain alone is worth over a billion pounds a year. Worldwide it is worth more than £18 billion. Its products range from diet books and slimming magazines to slimming clubs and exercise studios boasting machines combined with counters that tell you how many calories you are burning, and from slimming patches, creams, and other cures to the enormous range of "diet" drinks and low-fat, low-calorie, "slimming" foods available in your nearest supermarket or pharmacy.

Instead of being encouraged to eat real food, but less of it, we are led to believe by the manufacturers that eating more of certain foods—costly, slimming ones—will actually make us slim. New and ever-more-remarkable products are launched on the market, one of the very newest being "fat-free" fats. Proctor and Gamble's Olestra is a "fat-free" oil which has recently become available in the United States. This seemingly miraculous product is not metabolized; it passes straight through the system, so you get all the taste and cooking properties of ordinary fats or oils, but not the calories. You can gorge yourself on potato chips, fries, chocolate, and other fatty treats, but instead of settling on your hips, the fat content goes straight down the toilet. A dieter's dream come true, surely. The ultimate fantasy of a no-fat, low-calorie food orgasm! But the marketing of Olestra puts rather less emphasis on its side-effects, one of the more unpleasant of which is anal leakage. Rather a high price to pay for a slimming snack! And there are even more serious problems from a nutritional perspective: as it passes through the body, Olestra gathers with it valuable nutrients, including a lot of fat-soluble vitamins. Eating too much food high in fat—and indeed eating too much of any food—is conducive to weight gain, but eliminating fat altogether is extremely dangerous. We now know, for example, that essential fatty acids are vital to the development of our brains. So much for being able to eat more and weigh less.

The fact is that the claims made for diet foods by their manufacturers, and for diets by their authors or by slimming clubs, are highly misleading. Statistics show that more than 95 percent of people who lose weight by dieting put it all back on again, and more, as soon as they stop. Furthermore, many weight-loss programmes and commercial diets are gimmicky and nutritionally unsound. Diet clubs may sound a better option, but for every slimmer-of-the-year story, there is a story of last-year's slimmer-of-the-year who has not only regained all the weight she or he lost, but is fatter than before. Dieting is a complete con. Weight returns with a vengeance the minute you stop dieting because you go back to your usual eating patterns. Think of all the celebrities whose weight— often a barometer of their emotional health—goes up and down like a yoyo: Oprah Winfrey, Elizabeth Taylor, Kathleen Turner, Melanie Griffiths, Fergie, and Bill Clinton, to name but a few.

We all want to be thin, whether for our health, vanity, or self-esteem. But dieting is not the answer to losing weight. It just exacerbates the problem.

Dieting: The Wrong Prescription

Dieting not only makes you fat; it can seriously damage your health. The most serious risk associated with obesity is heart disease. This risk is increased, not reduced, by fluctuations in weight caused by dieting. Other hazards for dieters include an increased risk of osteoporosis, menstrual disorders, gallstones, and infertility. Fad diets are also dangerous from a nutritional point of view because they strictly limit the kinds and variety of foods you eat. As mentioned above, essential fatty acids are now recognized to be vital for our health, yet oily fish, the richest source, are on the "forbidden" list in the current best-selling diet book on the market. The food fascists who ban you from enjoying the rich variety of food and drink that is your right are doing you no favors.

Dieting is not just bad for your body; it is bad for your mind, too. Dieting leads to obsession, compulsion, and guilt, as well as depression and psychosis. Not only do you fail to lose weight, but worse still, you are liable to end up even fatter than before you started dieting. Many dieters develop an unhealthy cycle of starving and compulsive binge-eating along with the dieting mentality and massive weight fluctuations, or yoyo weight. Some dieters go on to develop serious eating disorders such as bulimia and anorexia nervosa which may require extensive medical and psychiatric treatment.

Different Diets, Same Results

You have only to look in your local bookstore or newsagent and see the shelves bulging with a bewildering variety of diet books and slimming magazines, all bearing the magical promise of a new sylphlike self, to realize how obsessed with dieting we as a nation are. But dieting is not just a national neurosis, it is an international one.

Diets go in fashions, and most rely on gimmicks: the low-carbohydrate, high-protein diet of yesteryear is replaced with the high-carbohydrate, low-fat diet of today; calorie-counting and egg and grapefruit diets are displaced by detoxification and food-combining diets. Most have little or no scientific credibility or nutritional value, and most dieters avidly try out every new diet that comes on the market in the vain hope that if the last one did not work, the next will. Of course if none do the trick—and usually none do, round the corner in the pharmacy or supermarket you can always find a range of expensive meal replacements—the fast route to *really* depressed taste buds!

Despite all their promises, and in spite of the fact that dieting has become a way of life for more and more of us, with around 60–70 percent of the female population in Britain and America currently on a diet, we are still getting fatter and fatter. Different as they may sound on the surface, all diets have similar effects. They deprive our natural desire and instinct for food. They damage our natural enjoyment of food and they have negative effects on our psyches.

Food Fascism

Diets "work" in the sense that they temporarily restrict your food consumption and therefore your calorie intake. Some diet books forbid fats, immediately ruling out not only butter, cookies, chips, cakes and chocolate but many kinds of fish, meat, nuts, and eggs which are normally considered highly nutritious. *The Food Combining Diet*, a bestseller by Kathryn Marsden, does not allow you to mix proteins and carbohydrates at the same meal and specifies an interval of several hours between meals of different types. You can wave goodbye, then, to traditional combinations such as meat or fish and two veg (where one vegetable consists of potatoes). Goodbye too to pizza, and to sprinkling Parmesan cheese on your pasta.

Goodbye legumes, peas, beans, and lentils: these curious blunders of nature contain high percentages of both protein and starch, which make them internally incompatible for human digestion. Never mind that, together with rice or other starches, they form the staple diet for much of the Asian population.

It is no wonder that most people cannot stick to a diet for long. Absurd or not, these diets inevitably fail because they deprive you of the foods that you love and need. People who diet are often food lovers with highly developed food libidos. They are not going to enjoy or be satisfied for long with the wimpy meals—like melba toast, cottage cheese, and a bit of salad with oil-free dressing—dreamed up by the diet dictators with their low or nonexistent food libidos. Not, at any rate, until they have gone so far down the dieting line that they have suppressed their taste buds almost out of existence and are heading towards food phobia. People with healthier appetites break their diets within a few days of starting, or a few weeks for those with more willpower. That is when the problems often begin.

The Dieting Mentality

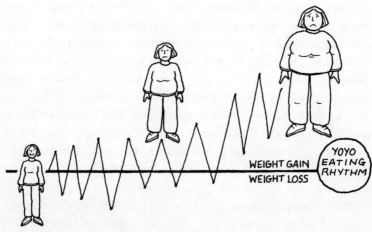

The dieting mentality

38

Not every dieter develops the dieting mentality—there are a few sane individuals who can flirt with a diet, maybe lose a few pounds, and lose interest in dieting too, realizing what a snare and a delusion it really is. Once we start dieting though, most of us get well and truly hooked, and firmly caught in the dieting trap.

The dieting mentality begins when you start to feel guilty after eating "sinful" foods and instead of just enjoying them, you wish you had not eaten. When you "cheat," and give in to eating a cream cake or a bit of chocolate, instead of acknowledging to yourself (as any non-dieter would if they bothered to think about it) that a few measly squares of chocolate or even an entire bar will make very little difference to your weight, and will not stop you carrying on with your diet or losing weight, you freak. The diet is over, the whole day is spoiled, and you have lost all control. To prove the point, you probably eat another cake or bar of chocolate. If you are a real food lover, then once triggered off by indulgent food, such as chocolate or potato chips, your excitable taste buds will be so aroused that you cannot stop eating until you have eaten enough chocolate or potato chips to peak, eating maybe three or five bars of chocolate, or the same number of bags of chips. But instead of enjoying it you feel weak-willed, piggish, and guilty. Doubly guilty, in fact, because not only have you eaten forbidden food, but you have eaten a lot of it. Full of remorse and self-reproach, you vow to start afresh the next day.

Each time, you go back to dieting with renewed vigor. Your weight begins to fluctuate by a few pounds—you lose a few and then gain a few, but nothing too drastic in the early stages of dieting. As you give in to your food cravings and your weight gently fluctuates, you increasingly train your will to abstain from the foods you love and crave, fight a constant battle with your body and impose on it unnatural eating regimes and behavior.

39

As guilt about "fattening" and "forbidden" foods takes hold, you develop a fear of food and its fattening effects, sometimes to the point of food phobia. And while you think about food more and more of the time, the pleasure you once derived from eating and drinking is diminished, if not destroyed, by your dieting mind. The guiltier you become, the more obsessively you diet and starve yourself.

Guilt, Food Obsession, and Compulsive Eating

The obsessive-compulsive guilt cycle

If you are not prone to obsessions or compulsive behavior in any other aspect of your life, chances are you will not develop an obsessive relationship with food or compulsive eating behavior. But for many people, dieting leads to obsession—and there is no such thing as sensible dieting among obsessive people. If you have even a slightly obsessive personality, as most dieters do, as time goes by you diet more and more, harder and harder.

The more obsessively you diet, the more obsessively you think about food and the greater your compulsion to eat. Inevitably, if you are on a low-calorie or starvation diet all day or for several days, your blood sugar falls to the point where your body is literally screaming for food. When you eventually eat, you go berserk and binge. Then you feel guilty and starve, then binge, then starve, and so on. Your weight begins to swing wildly—you can lose 7 lb in a week and put it all back in a day.

Trapped in a vicious cycle of guilt, obsession, and compulsion, you alternate between dieting, bingeing, and starving as your weight yoyos along with your dieting mind. Obsession with food can lead to serious eating disorders such as anorexia nervosa and bulimia, discussed in Chapter 1.

Compulsive Exercising

Without any doubt, regular exercise is a good thing for most people. It keeps you fit and, like most of the medical profession, I am very much in favor of a moderate program of light exercise, consisting of activities such as swimming, walking, and yoga. People who are very overweight or obese, and unused to taking exercise, should, of course, build up gradually, preferably in consultation with their doctor or another qualified health specialist.

However, I am against the use of strenuous exercise as a way of dieting. Like any other form of dieting, it can become an unhealthy obsession in the quest to lose weight and stay in shape. When it becomes an addiction, exercise is neither enjoyable, nor good for your health. Compulsive exercising often goes hand-in-hand with eating disorders, sometimes replacing the eating disorder as the sufferer from anorexia or bulimia "recovers" from one disorder only to replace it with another.

People who get hooked on exercise—and experts believe that more than half of all "fitness" enthusiasts are addicts—run, step-dance, do aerobics, weight-train and, generally work out harder and harder, and more and more frequently, until gradually their whole lives revolve around it, just as obsessive dieters' lives revolve around food. Compelled to exercise vigorously, often several times a day, for several hours a day, fitness addicts panic when they are unable to exercise even for a day or two, terrified that they will put on weight and get out of shape.

Fitness junkies have to be virtually dead or unable to move before they miss their workouts, runs, and training sessions. Because endorphins suppress the sensation of pain, compulsive exercisers continue to exercise even through the painful fractures, torn ligaments, and muscle injuries they frequently sustain, risking permanent damage. When they really cannot exercise for a while—if, for example, they break a leg—they inevitably do put on a lot of weight and get withdrawal symptoms.

Compulsive exercising, like dieting, is not the answer to losing weight. There are all sorts of good reasons to exercise, whether daily or several times a week, so long as you do not do so fanatically as a way to avoid the food your body requires. The only way to lose weight permanently is to learn the art of eating.

Never Say Diet Again!

Dieting may contribute to healthy profit margins for big multinationals as well as smaller business concerns, but it contributes nothing to *your* health. In fact it is much more likely to damage your health, both physical and mental.

Dieting demoralizes you because you feel guilty when you eat the food you love; it demeans you because you feel greedy when you "cheat"; worst of all, it destroys your self-esteem. You completely lose your confidence as you not only fail to lose weight, but gain weight and become fatter than when you began dieting.

You can now begin to see how dieting trains your mind to go against the natural flow of the body, which is to eat and drink at certain times of day in order to function well. Dieting is like swimming against the tide: your mind and body flow in opposite directions, creating a build-up of tension which cannot be sustained. This is why diets fail dieters.

Dieting is at best an unnatural way to slim, resulting in temporary or, for the lucky five percent, longer-term weight loss. For the rest of us, the best that can be said about dieting is that it makes slim people fat, and fat people fatter, as they become increasingly neurotic and obsessive about food and their weight. At its worst, dieting drags you towards debilitating and potentially fatal conditions such as anorexia and bulimia.

3

The Naked Body: What Shape Are You?

One of the first things we notice about people is their size and shape. Long and lean, short and stocky, shapely and voluptuous, small and delicate, large and shapeless, thin and emaciated—the combinations and permutations are infinite. Walk down any street or into your local supermarket and you will see an endless variety of shapes, sizes, and heights.

Sharply in contrast to this rich assortment of types are the monomorphic models featured in women's magazines—every one a tall, leggy, superslim size 6 or less. Because society's perception is that clothes generally look better on tall, slim girls, fashion displays one sort of image instead of reflecting the diversity of normal shapes and sizes. So, despite the preference of many for feminine curves, fashion-conscious women and girls do their best to lose weight and rearrange their shapes to fit current ideals, trying to become slim but sensual, long and lean with shapely breasts, or straight up and down flat-chested, according to the latest thin whim of the fashion elite. But in trying to emulate the perfect size 6 figures which stare out from the pages of glossy magazines, we often forget to take into consideration the shape we were born with.

Nobody is born fat or destined to become so, but our basic build or body type *is* genetically determined and cannot be altered even by obsessive dieting and constant exercise, with all their attendant risks. Brainwashed by fashion's fantasy images of superslim perfection, women often confuse their genetic body type with being fat and attempt to remold themselves into shapes they can only aspire to, making themselves prone to eating disorders and obsession in the process.

Basic Body Types

Despite the infinite variety of human shapes and sizes, there are three main groups into which we all fall—the ectomorph, the mesomorph, and the endomorph—even though we may not be perfect examples of the type. Different people are attracted to different types, and different cultures admire different shapes and amounts of flesh. The slim, angular bodies of Western film stars are often shown as plumper than they actually are on posters in India advertising the films, because their standards of beauty and attractiveness differ from ours. The ideal for Eastern and Middle Eastern women is to be well-rounded or even plump, whereas in most of Europe and the States it is a case of the thinner, the better (within reason). But thin or fat, the three basic shapes are universal, as are the main subgroups within each of those.

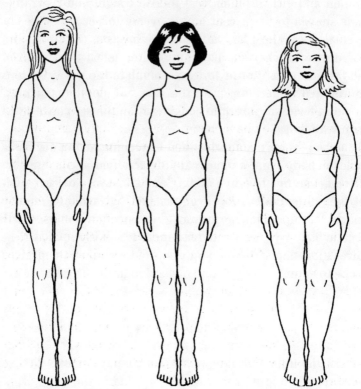

The three basic body types—ectomorph, mesomorph, and endomorph

The Ectomorph

Although she struggled for much of her life with eating disorders, Audrey Hepburn, famous beauty and film star of the 1950s and 1960s, nevertheless epitomizes the perfect ectomorphic shape—long, lean and elegant, the model type most women would love to be. Twiggy, Gwyneth Paltrow, and Kate Moss are all celebrated ectomorphs, models, more famous for the shape of their bodies than for anything else. On the male side, a perfect example of the species is Clint Eastwood, and other well-known male ectomorphs include Ralph Fiennes, Jeremy Irons, Mick Jagger, Anthony Edwards, Tiger Woods, and Jim Carrey. The classic ectomorph is tall, 5 ft 7 in or over for women, 5 ft 11 in and upwards in the case of men, but like the other two types, ectomorphs can be tall, medium, or short.

The typical ectomorph is slim and long-limbed with little body fat, what they have being evenly distributed and inconspicuous. Female ectomorphs have small but shapely breasts and theirs has been the most fashionable figure this century, the one dieters strive to attain. The superwaif ideal personified by Twiggy in the 1960s and more recently by Kate Moss in the 1990s caused a furore, giving rise to much debate and speculation over the connection between such role models and the rise in eating disorders such as anorexia among young women.

If they put on a bit of weight, the ectomorph's slim limbs easily absorb the surplus pounds. A weight gain of seven pounds will simply make them look well, and often goes unnoticed by others. Seemingly able to eat whatever they like without gaining weight, they are often the envy of their dieting friends.

The Mesomorph

Sophia Loren, film star and international sex symbol, is a perfect example of the female mesomorphic shape—athletic but voluptuous. Charlton Heston, another sex symbol of his day, is the male equivalent—strong, athletic, and muscular. Other famous mesomorphs include Princess Di, Madonna, Liz Hurley, Cindy Crawford and Jane Fonda; Arnold Schwarzenegger, David Hasselhoff, and George Clooney.

The typical mesomorph is well-built, muscular, and robust, with more fat than the typical ectomorph, but less than the endomorph. Female mesomorphs are usually well endowed, with good breasts, and their fat is often concentrated on the hips and shoulders. When they put on weight it is more noticeable than it is for ectomorphs, and they often look top-heavy when they are out of shape. An extra seven pounds will give them a rather stocky appearance, especially if they are on the short side.

The Endomorph

Marilyn Monroe, 1950s film star and the world's greatest sex goddess, was the quintessential endomorph, perfect of her type—rounded and curvaceous, a well-proportioned size 14–16 with an hourglass figure. Kelsey Grammer, who plays Frasier, is the perfect example of a male endomorph. Other well-known endomorphs include Brigitte Bardot, Joan Collins, Oprah Winfrey, Elizabeth Taylor, the Queen of England, Fergie, and Hillary Clinton; Bill Clinton, Richard Simmons, and Matt Damon.

The typical endomorph has a fuller figure, with a naturally higher fat content than the other two body types. Female endomorphs have comparatively short limbs, large rounded breasts and hips, and they go in at the waist—womanly curves in all the right places, when in shape. Glamor and sex appeal in the 1950s and early 1960s were defined by the likes of Marilyn Monroe and Brigitte Bardot. Statistics were vital and female contours were rounded and full. But although the endomorph is still considered the perfect shape for women in many non-Western cultures, and Marilyn Monroe's enduring appeal is proof that many still prefer voluptuous curves to the svelte models of today, the endomorph is generally no longer fashionable in the West. However, the rise of British model Sophie Dahl, now much in vogue with her voluptuous curves, bucks the trend for superwaifs.

When endomorphs put on weight it is difficult to conceal. An additional seven pounds makes them look fat. Because their rounded shapes expose any excess weight far more obviously than do the other two shapes, overweight and obesity appears more widespread among endomorphs.

Out of Shape

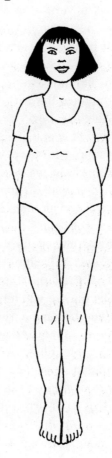

Pear and apple shapes

When slim people put on weight, their natural shape becomes distorted. They lose the lines that reveal their basic body type —ectomorph, mesomorph or endomorph, and become either pear- or apple-shaped. Pears have a small waist measurement in comparison with their hip measurement, whereas apples have a high waist-to-hip ratio. The distribution of fat on your body is, like your natural body type, genetically determined; apples with their rounded tummies and relatively slim hips will never become pears, with their fatter tummies and heavier buttocks. But while ectomorphs can often put on 14 pounds before they lose their shape, endomorphs have only to put on a few pounds before they become out of shape. Mesomorphs lie somewhere in between the two, but are usually out of shape once they are more than seven pounds above their ideal weight.

When they gain weight, most women develop the familiar pear shape, with excess fat settling on their hips and thighs. Men almost always become apples—their pot bellies hanging out of their waistbands in rhythm with the speed at which they swill down their beers and the size of their burgers. Famous pot-bellies include Pavarotti, while former slimmies who have now gone to pot include Jack Nicholson, Roger Moore, and Al Pacino. Well-known female apples include the Queen of England, Barbara Cartland, and Oprah Winfrey, whereas Fergie, when out of shape, is the more typical pear. When you become seriously overweight or obese, fat settles all over your body and you are neither apple nor pear, just out of shape. Famously out of shape are Roseanne Barr, John Goodman, and John Madden.

Overweight apples are at a higher risk of heart disease, high blood pressure, and diabetes than pears.

Is There an Ideal Weight?

Many doctors, slimming clinics and clubs, and dieting products set target weights for dieters to work toward. These do not take into account different body types and are often designed to sell products and services at inflated prices. They are also a causative factor in the development of the dieting mentality, as dieters obsessively try to hit their target weight daily, feeling guilty when they fail to do so. In fact, people's weight naturally fluctuates and women's weight especially, according to which phase of their menstrual cycle they are currently going through. Many women experience an increase in weight of several pounds, and sometimes much more, peaking a few days before their period begins.

Shape is a much more accurate way of assessing whether you are the right weight. We all think in terms of shape rather than weight—we do not describe people's appearance in terms of their weight, but in terms of their height and build. Target weights are static measurements, more appropriate for inanimate objects than living, breathing bodies, which secrete and excrete, their weight fluctuating in rhythm with their natural functions. Shape, on the other hand, is dynamic, allowing for the natural flow and movement of your body's individual rhythms.

It is unrealistic to keep to an exact weight, but useful to think in terms of a weight *range* appropriate to your height and shape. You are within your correct weight range when you feel good and look good. The most useful guide to your correct weight is provided by the body mass index (BMI), which gives an acceptable weight range for any given height.

The Body Mass Index (BMI)

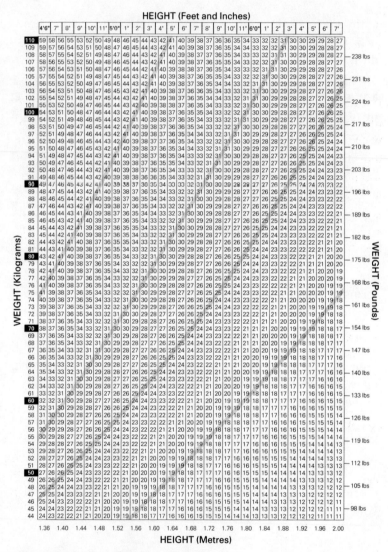

Adapted from J. S. Gallow in *Obesity and Related Diseases*

Body mass index table

52

41 – 59 = very obese
31 – 41 = obese
26 – 30 = overweight
19 – 25 = healthy
11 – 18 = underweight

Devised in 1871 by a Belgian astronomer named Dr. Quetelet, the body mass index (BMI) not only gives acceptable ranges of weight for any given height, but can be used as a diagnostic tool in assessing degrees of overweight and obesity, under-weight and emaciation. Your body mass index covers a fluct-uating weight of between five and seven pounds, and when you increase your BMI by one whole integer, say from 22 to 23, you will have changed your naked shape and it will become noticeable. Your body mass index is calculated by a simple formula—your weight in kilograms (wearing light or indoor clothing, and no shoes) divided by your height in metres squared.

How to calculate your BMI

$$\text{BMI} = \frac{\text{weight in kilograms}}{\text{height in metres} \times \text{height in metres}}$$

EXAMPLE:

Weight = 136 pounds = 61 kilograms
Height = 5 feet 5 inches = 1.65 metres

$$\text{BMI} = \frac{61}{1.65 \times 1.65} = 22.4$$

You do not need a calculator to work out your BMI. The table opposite will do this for you.

The medical establishment regards anyone with a BMI within the range 19—25 as being of normal or desirable weight. Those with a BMI between 25 and 30 are regarded as overweight, those between 30 and 40 as obese, and anyone over 40 very obese. Those with a BMI between 15 and 19 are regarded as being underweight, while a BMI of 15 or below is emaciated. Those with a BMI in the last category are almost always anorexic, unless they are suffering physical or mental illnesses which have involved severe weight loss.

Although the BMI is an extremely useful indicator of weight problems, it does not take into account body types. A BMI of 25, the higher end of the medically acceptable or desirable range, is actually very overweight for the ectomorph, and slightly overweight even for mesomorphs. Having a petite Chinese frame, with small bones, and being an ectomorph, I was 40 pounds overweight and completely out of shape when my BMI rose to 25, soon after I arrived in the UK.

For further accuracy and for my own use in my clinics, I have subdivided the "desirable" weight range, taking into account the three main body types:

For the *ectomorph* the ideal BMI lies between 19 and 21.99*
For the *mesomorph* the ideal BMI is between 22 and 23.99
For the *endomorph* the ideal BMI is between 24 and 26.

These subdivisions work extremely well for all my clients and take weight and shape obsessions off their minds. Those who are extremely overweight or obese work first of all towards a BMI of 26 or less, then, when their natural body shape becomes apparent, this may be revised downward.

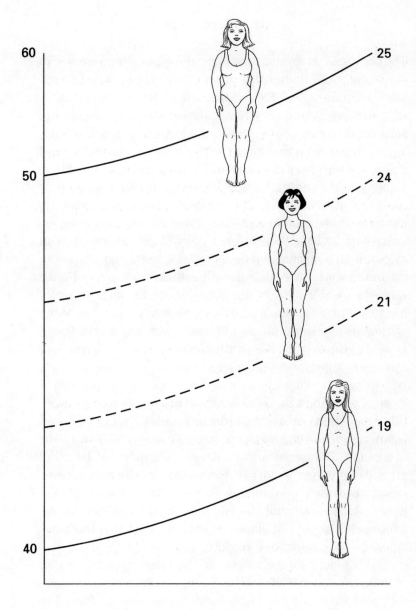

Body mass index and body types

The Body Trap

The pressures on women to be slim, and especially on women in the public eye—think of Princess Di, Fergie, Hillary Clinton, Oprah Winfrey, and Rikki Lake, all of whom have visibly slimmed down since they first came under the spotlight—are stronger than ever before, leading many women to drastic dieting as they attempt to change their shapes in pursuit of the ideal figure. With fashion icons like Kate Moss—a role model for many young girls—featuring in all the popular press, skinniness is more in vogue than ever, and an almost prepubescent shape is portrayed as being the norm. But trying to emulate the super-waif shape, which Kate Moss, a very slight ectomorph, can maintain on a normal diet, leads only to illness and obsession.

In the world of modeling, eating disorders are rife. Unlike Kate Moss—or Twiggy in the 1960s—not all models are ecto-morphs; and not all supermodels are naturally superthin. Many are natural mesomorphs, and have to virtually starve them-selves to keep their bodies, which are of course their livelihood, at a size 6. Supermodel Yasmin Le Bon has been known to faint with hunger at photo shoots, and used to exist on a daily diet of a cup of soup and a bar of chocolate in order to keep her shape. Other models live on a diet consisting largely of black coffee and cigarettes, throwing up when they succumb to eating—or overeating. The former model Margaux Hemingway, beautiful granddaughter of the novelist Ernest Hemingway, was a meso-morph. Because she wanted to change into an ectomorph she dieted obsessively, until she became victim to bulimia as she alternately starved and binged. Eventually, like her grandfather before her, she committed suicide.

Alicia Machado, the 19-year-old Venezuelan beauty queen who became Miss Universe in 1996, threw up, starved her-self, and exercised for eight hours a day to transform her naturally endomorphic shape into the sylphlike body with which she gained the title. At 5 ft 8 in and weighing just under 112 lb, she had scarcely eaten in the weeks leading up to her crowning moment and was seriously underweight. Having won the title, she began to eat again with the result that she put on weight. She made more headlines—'Queen of Flab'— for the weight she gained during her brief reign as Miss Universe than she had for winning the title in the first place. But although not overweight by normal standards, her body simply does not conform to the standards set by the fashion industry. No matter how much she diets and starves herself, with her full breasts and shapely curves she can never become a stick insect.

When you try to change your body from its natural shape to another through obsessive dieting and exercise, you are falling into the body trap. When you get caught in the body trap you abuse your body, disrupting its natural rhythms and eating habits, imposing on it eating regimes you cannot keep, all too often ending up by purging and vomiting when you fail to keep to the impossible targets you set yourself. Critical media attention and cruel headlines such as the ones earned by Alicia Machado have led many a celebrity into the body trap. Being a constant target for the paparazzi, and inevitably sometimes caught in an off moment or after putting on a few pounds, people can easily become fixated with their shape, and with trying to change their shape. Diana, Princess of Wales, the world's most photographed woman, was a mesomorph who tried to change her body into that of an ectomorph through dieting. The price was bulimia. However, at the time of her tragic and untimely death, she had recovered and was back in perfect shape. Benazir Bhutto, erstwhile prime minister of Pakistan and a typical mesomorph, also dieted until she became bulimic trying to attain her ideal ectomorphic shape, becoming periodically very slim before regaining weight in the typical yoyo pattern suffered by many obsessive dieters.

But though it is they who set the often impossible standards for the rest of us to follow, falling into the body trap is not something that happens mainly to models and celebrities. It is what happens when you become an obsessive dieter, as discussed in Chapter 2. If you are caught in the body trap, you develop a distorted image of your own body and lose all sense of proportion. When you feel fat you see yourself as much fatter than you really are. You have what I call a fat mind. Obsessive dieters, who are almost by definition neurotic about their weight and shape, invariably believe themselves to be substantially fatter than they are, with particular areas of their bodies —thighs top the bill—as focal points for their self-loathing and disgust. I was no exception in my fat, dieting days. My great obsession was my "moon" face—we Chinese have a tendency to develop round faces when we overeat. If I so much as ate a single bar of chocolate, the forbidden food I could not live without, no matter how I tried, I would immediately feel fatter. With my fat mindset, I could actually feel my face expanding as the chocolate disappeared down my throat. Former actress and fitness guru Jane Fonda, a self-confessed bulimic, has—or had —a similar mindset. While thousands of dieters strove to be just like her, she herself never felt as thin as she wished to be and actually admitted to hating her own body.

There are two sides to every coin, of course, and on the opposite side of the body trap coin to the dieters lie the beanpoles who long for a cleavage and curves. Stunning clad in their designer dresses, they feel sadly lacking when they peel them off and reveal their flat chests and non-existent bottoms. Paula Yates, for example, a typical ectomorph, famously had breast implants—augmentation of the breast is still the most popular form of cosmetic surgery, despite worries of associated health risks.

It is a fact that women have always tried to alter their shapes to conform with current fashions, with the help of a little strategic padding here and there, or with bodices and corsets—standard undergarments for women not so long ago. But short of plastic surgery, striving to change your naked shape into a different model is as futile and damaging as trying to become someone you are not. And there are limits to what plastic surgery can do for you too, even if you are willing to go that far. I am totally in favor of keeping in shape and making the most of your body—your own uniquely shaped body, whichever main type it falls into, but it is pointless and dangerous to fight against your bone structure and natural body type.

Love Yourself, Love Your Body—It's The Only One You Will Ever Have

There really is no one perfect shape or figure, despite the best efforts of the fashion industry, with its preference for anorexic bone bags, to convince us otherwise. But the bag of bones that looks terrific in a big thick jumper with a quilted coat on top can look painfully thin in a swimsuit or naked. While the fashion industry concerns itself with the shape of clothes on a body, I am concerned with the shape of the body beneath the clothes, and with helping men and women to reach *their* perfect shape, not someone else's. Your perfect shape is the one at which you look and feel your best, and it is unique to you, just as Cindy Crawford's shape is uniquely hers, and nobody else's.

To look and feel good, you need to discover and accept your own body type, and learn how to eat in accordance with your natural rhythms, maintaining the right weight for your shape and height. The rest of this book is devoted to helping you find out why you are overweight if you are, and to explaining the principles and practice of eating orgasmically, the art of eating naturally and keeping in shape.

4

Why Are You Overweight?
The Myths and the Facts

You only have to look at slim people's expressions when they see fatties tucking in to know they suspect the obvious—that overweight and obese people simply eat and drink too much. The disdain and disapproval of those who believe that if you are not pencil thin you have no right to eat anything other than chopped apples and undressed lettuce leaves adds to the misery of those of us who love food and wage constant warfare with our waistlines. Most of us have tried every which way to lose weight, but despair of diets. We have healthy appetites, but we are not greedy and so we feel hurt by the tacit criticism. Surely being fat must be something to do with our metabolism, our genes, hormones running wild, or fluid retention?

Yes and no. As I will explain later, it is certainly not true that all fat or overweight people are greedy, yet the slimmies are right in believing that fat people overeat and drink, as those at the cutting edge of research have now shown. With the exception of one or two rare diseases, the unpalatable truth is that fat people simply do eat much more than thin ones.

It is no coincidence that the home of obesity is America, a country in which more than 30 percent of the population is officially classified as obese. Size is everything in America – whether it is the size of your car or the size of your girth. Food portions served in the average American restaurant are outsize by the standards of anywhere else, as are the sodas and cartons of popcorn sold in cinemas, and the giant packs of snacks, sweets, fast foods, convenience foods, and other foods and drinks sold in American supermarkets. The rest of the Western world, and even the Eastern hemisphere, are catching up fast, and so are their obesity statistics. But I strongly believe that *no one is born fat nor destined to become fat.*

However upset we may be to learn that it is our eating habits and the amount we eat that make us fat, the good news is that we can acquire new eating behavior and reverse the problems of overweight and obesity caused by our present habits. But before you can do so, especially if you are a veteran dieter, you need to understand why it is that you have developed, often over your entire lifetime, your current eating habits, and what exactly the processes that lead to overweight and obesity are. In understanding these lies the solution. But first I will expose the myths of overweight and obesity.

The Myths of Obesity

New clients I see in my clinics come up with every conceivable reason for the fact that they are overweight. The bigger the patient, the better the reason or excuse: being fat runs in the family; they have just given up smoking; business entertaining in the form of a daily routine of eggs and bacon breakfasts, three-course lunches and dinners; it is a result of hormonal imbalances or taking HRT; food is a release from pent-up emotions or a high-pressure lifestyle. But believing themselves to have a slow metabolism is by far and away the most common reason volunteered by my patients for being over-weight. They assure me they are on a constant diet, eating like a sparrow, but never able to lose weight. So it *must* be due to their metabolism. Because this belief—that at least some of us are doomed never to lose weight because of sluggish metabolisms—is so widespread, I shall discuss it in detail.

Metabolism

Your metabolic rate is the speed at which your body uses up the energy (calories) it receives from the food you eat, once broken down into a usable form. Your basal metabolic rate (BMR) is the amount of energy used when you are at rest, for breathing, blood circulation and so on, and is the largest component—about 75 percent—of your total energy expenditure. Extra energy in the form of calories is required to digest and process food, and to keep warm. Physical activity also eats up energy—anything from about 400 to 1000 or more kilocalories a day depending on how active you are (1 kilocalorie = 1000 calories).

If the energy value of the food you eat (your calorie intake) exceeds your energy output (the calories you burn up) then the body will lay down the extra energy in the form of fat and you will put on weight.

Some diseases cause your metabolic rate to rise—a high temperature is an indication of this, and certain drugs can also speed up your metabolism. On the other hand, an underactive thyroid slows down your metabolism and weight gain is often put down to this. However, despite the ingrained belief of most overweight people and many doctors, recent research has conclusively established that fat people actually have higher, not lower, metabolic rates than thin people. This is because overweight people not only have more fat, they also have more metabolically active lean tissue, which is needed to support the additional fat. BMR can now be fairly accurately predicted (to within plus or minus 15 percent) for any given body weight, and has been found to increase in proportion to weight. And although there are individual differences, those with a BMR a bit lower than predicted are just as likely to be thin as fat. So, for example, a woman weighing 125 pounds (55.5 kilograms) will have a BMR in the region of 1310 kilocalories a day, whereas a woman weighing 210 pounds (95 kilograms) will have a BMR of about 1620 kilocalories a day, about 24 percent higher than the lighter woman. The BMR for men, weight for weight, is a little higher than for women.

But fat people are less active than slim ones, are they not? So surely the higher BMR of fat people is balanced out by less energy being burned up through physical activity? Until recently it had proved difficult to measure the energy expended in physical activity, but new techniques developed at the Dunn Clinical Nutrition Centre in Cambridge, England, have enabled researchers to make accurate assessments with surprising findings. They have found that in addition to having a higher BMR than thin people, fat people use up much more energy than thin ones doing the same physical activities. This is because most activities are weight-dependent, so, for example when they eat, fat people burn up more calories than thin ones because of the greater amount of energy needed to move heavy rather than thin arms. Other everyday activities such as moving, getting dressed, and going up and down stairs all require much more of the fat person than the thin one. The sheer weight of very fat and obese people can sap their energy to such a degree that they feel tired all the time and movement is seriously inhibited. To go back to the previous example, adding the energy expended through thermogenesis and physical activity to the BMR, the total energy expenditure of an averagely active 126-pound woman is around 2000 kilocalories, and of an averagely active 210-pound woman around 2430 kilocalories.

Although nobody, and myself least of all, is saying that all fat people are gluttons, the fact is that those who say they hardly eat but still cannot lose weight are usually underestimating—sometimes grossly—the amount of food they consume. It is simply a myth that some people can eat vast quantities of food and still stay slim. The thin people who you see eating to their heart's content probably *do* eat whatever they want—but they recognize when they have had enough and they stop. They eat orgasmically, in fact. They employ the art of compensation either instinctively or having trained themselves to do so, paying back for a huge meal by eating little beforehand or at the following meal.

But what, you may be thinking, about the effect of dieting on metabolism? Is it not true that when you diet your metabolic rate goes down to compensate? The body interprets a sudden drop in the quantity of food it normally processes as a starvation alert, so it uses whatever food resources it gets very efficiently, and conserves its reserves of fat as far as possible. We all know by now that dieting makes you fat. Surely this must be one of the reasons why.

This is true to the extent that when you eat, your metabolic rate goes up as you digest and process the food, and as you gain weight the number of calories you burn daily also goes up, as I have explained above. Conversely, on a starvation diet your metabolic rate goes down because no energy is being used in processing food. Genuine famine victims who face prolonged shortage of food are uniformly thin, and their metabolic rates are likely to be very low.

The myth that one's metabolism is to blame for excess pounds can and should be laid firmly to rest. Metabolism is not the culprit, and the belief that it is serves only to undermine the motivation of overweight people who believe they are fighting an unbeatable metabolic enemy. With the exception of very rare cases with congenital diseases, no one is born or destined to be fat. All overweight and obese people can lose weight, without giving up the foods they adore, when they retrain their eating habits by eating orgasmically and learning how to eat—and drink—less, without feeling deprived.

Genes

There is no denying that being overweight tends to run in families, and much research has been directed into establishing whether this is the result of genetic inheritance or whether it is to do with the family environment and lifestyle. We know that eating habits are highly conditioned, and develop from an early age. So if you have been conditioned throughout your life to eat more than you need to, brought up to "eat it all up" and "leave a clean plate," or rewarded for good behavior by candy and other edible treats, then you will have developed fat eating behaviour and will be out of shape. But is there a genetic component too?

When it comes to your natural shape—ectomorph, mesomorph, or endomorph, tall or short—there is no doubt that genes have everything to do with it. However much you diet and exercise, you cannot alter your basic framework. Research studies on families, adopted and foster children, and identical and nonidentical twins have established that our genes also determine where on our bodies excess fat is stored—whether you become a pear or an apple when you gain weight. But although *distribution* of fat is genetically programed, the research on twins shows that the *amount* of fat on our bodies —whether we are fat or thin—has nothing to do with our genes. Identical twins, sharing the same genes, will put on weight in exactly the same way, having exactly the same shape when they are the same weight. But there can be a difference of thirty pounds in weight between them.

"It's All Water Retention"

So insist some of my larger clients when they walk into the clinic. But although water retention can cause temporary weight gain (see below), it is never the whole story. In fact, the heavier you are, the less water you retain, proportionately. While water makes up about 70 percent of the mass of the average man, it accounts for only 50–55 percent of a woman's. Very obese women may have a water content as low as 40 percent. This is because women's bodies have a greater fat content—responsible for the more curvaceous female form —than men's, and fat tissue does not store water.

Excessive water retention may be caused by heart disease, kidney failure, and some forms of cancer, serious illnesses which are unlikely to be confused with overweight or obesity. In the absence of these, water retention is usually due to the monthly hormonal dance of the menstrual cycle, or to hormone replacement therapy (HRT).

Feeling Fat and Bloated

Some days you wake up feeling fat and bloated, at least seven pounds heavier, and—horror of horrors—the scales prove you right! You cannot get into your favorite jeans, the waistbands of all your skirts are too tight, and you feel lumpy and unattractive. Face, fingers, ankles, and feet may also swell up, causing puffy eyes, making rings harder to put on or take off, and shoes feel tight. If you are having a fat day, chances are that you are in the week leading up to your period.

Three or four days before your period begins hormone levels peak, and around this time high hormone levels cause your body to retain more water and salt. Most women gain three or four pounds as a result of water retention in the week or two before a period. To make matters worse, you probably have an increased appetite as a result of the hormone imbalance and feel more inclined to nibble than usual. You may have cravings for particular foods—salty foods like potato chips, as well as chocolate. If you have a high food libido, then once your taste buds are stimulated by nibbling you will get into the mood to eat and may find it difficult to stop.

Fat days arising from fluctuating hormone levels hit all women from time to time, but they do not last and you can help yourself by drinking less and cutting down on salt just before and during a period. You may gain weight, but you will not get out of shape unless you continuously overeat. Using the quiet rhythm, you can control and suppress your taste buds. Eating orgasmically and employing the art of compensation when your estrogen levels go down again will quickly bring your weight back to normal.

Menopause and HRT

Menopause is the permanent cessation of monthly periods, which can occur gradually or abruptly as a result of a decline and changes in the balance of the sex hormones. Many menopausal women complain of weight gain and fluid retention, but there is no physiological basis for this, although hormonal changes can lead to hot flashes, night sweats, and a dry vagina. Emotional symptoms may include moodiness, irritability, depression, weepiness, and insomnia.

Many of these symptoms can be reversed by hormone replacement therapy (HRT), which commonly consists of some form of estrogen, or a combination of estrogen and progesterone. However these hormones can also cause salt and water retention, as well as increase your appetite. If your taste buds are highly arousable, then once you start nibbling you just cannot stop. You can all too easily get into the mood to eat, permanently, and you will put on weight and get out of shape if you do not regain control by eating orgasmically.

Like premenstrual women, women on HRT need to restrict their salt and fluid intake to minimize the effects of water retention.

So Why Do We Overeat?

The simple reason why we get out of shape is, as we have seen, eating and drinking too much. But what we really need to understand is why we overeat and what the processes that lead to obesity are.

There are three main patterns or cycles of eating behavior which lead either on their own or in combination to putting on weight—the *mood-to-eat cycle*, failure to experience the *hunger cycle,* and the *obsessive-compulsive guilt cycle.* Once you discover which of these cycles contribute to your weight problem, you will be able slim down and get into shape.

But first we will look at the biological mechanisms that control the amount of food that slim or normal weight people eat.

Hunger, Appetite, and the Hunger–Satiety Mechanism

Some lucky people, without dieting or constantly watching their weight, seem to stay slim, effortlessly maintaining much the same weight from one year to the next throughout their adult life, except during bouts of illness or through pregnancy. They seem to have a built-in mechanism which automatically switches off their appetite once they have eaten the right amount of the right foods—foods of sufficient variety and balance to meet their nutritional needs, and in quantities that match their energy expenditure. So even though slim people vary quite considerably in the amount of energy they use up— in other words, they have different metabolic rates—their bodies seem to recognize this and adjust.

Actually, these people are no different from the rest of us. We all possess a natural braking mechanism, the hunger-satiety mechanism (HSM), which controls our food intake and tells us when we need to eat and when we have eaten enough and should stop. This feedback mechanism is extremely sensitive, however, and eating habits which we gradually form during our lifetimes can override its messages. The natural rhythm for the body is to be hungry…full…hungry…full (*see diagram page 90*). When you have not eaten for several hours, and your stomach is empty, the brain sends out hunger signals, giving you a sensation of emptiness. As you eat, your hunger subsides until, when you have eaten enough, your HSM signals you to stop. Hunger is replaced by a feeling of satiety or fullness.

You cannot control hunger and the need for sustenance any more than you can control tiredness and the need for sleep. Hunger is a purely physiological, unconditioned phenomenon which lets us know when our bodies require fuel, and makes us want to eat.

69

Appetite, in contrast to hunger, is a psychological phenomenon. Closely related to our taste buds, appetite is the desire for food and the enjoyment of certain kinds of foods. It is highly conditioned, or learned, and highly adaptable. Appetite develops from an early age and is very much influenced by our family and cultural environments. We learn to love the smells, tastes, and presentation of typical foods we are served—pasta, spicy foods, or burgers and hot dogs. When we go on vacation abroad, the more adventurous of us —and most food lovers—will try the local cuisine, but many people are so conditioned in their tastes that they cannot bear to be parted from their usual fare for even a day. Many American tourists will do their best to procure an eggs and bacon breakfast followed by a burger and fries for lunch, even in the most exotic of places, rather than try out the native cuisine, however delicious.

Ideally, hunger and appetite work together, ensuring that we satisfy our taste buds while eating a sufficient variety of food to fulfill our bodies' needs, and enough—but not too much —of it. Unfortunately our hunger, appetite, and stomachs are not always satisfied by the same amounts of the same foods, particularly if we have very demanding taste buds, and so we overeat. If you grow accustomed to overeating, and ignoring the signals sent out by the hunger-satiety mechanism, the mechanism falls into disuse and fails to prevent you from eating beyond the requirements of your body.

Fortunately the HSM can be reactivated by consciously regulating and controlling the amount of food you eat.

The Hunger Cycle

As explained in the section on metabolism (*see page 62*), the food you eat is converted into energy. This is used to maintain the physiological bodily functions which keep us alive and breathing, to keep us warm and in physical activity. Any surplus food is stored as fat. In the normal course of things, when your stomach is empty, the HSM sends out a hunger signal and you eat. The body's natural food rhythm is to alternate between being hungry and being full or satisfied (*see diagram page 90*). Naturally slim people normally complete this cycle three times a day, regulating their food intake and weight in the process without thinking about it. They eat when they feel hungry because they do not feel the need to lose weight and they regularly experience the hunger cycle.

When you allow yourself to feel hungry as you wait for your next meal, and do not eat in between meals, then the energy your body needs will be metabolized from your reserves of fat. So hunger is losing weight, and the more time you spend hungry, the more weight you will lose—so long as you do not get so hungry that you lose control and binge when you do eat.

The converse is also true. If you never feel hungry, you will not lose weight. Many overweight people rarely or never achieve the hunger cycle, often as a result of a childhood upbringing in a home where food flowed freely and developing the habit of overeating from an early age. We all know that eggs, bacon and pancakes with syrup for breakfast washed down with milky coffee is hardly a recipe for rapid weight loss, but in reality people have very different ideas of what a "normal" amount to eat is and those who have been accustomed from an early age to large portions accept them as the norm. Conditioned to avoid the sensation of hunger by eating large, nutritious meals which are not fully digested and

71

metabolized by the next mealtime, or by snacking in between meals, they can no longer accept or tolerate being hungry. In the absence of the regulating action of the HSM, they eat more and more because they never feel full. But the more you eat, the more your appetite and eating capacity increase. If you never allow yourself to feel hungry, and your stomach is never empty, you do not achieve the hunger cycle. Consequently you not only find it impossible to lose weight, but you gain weight.

Failure to experience hunger is one of the reasons dieters do not lose weight. Continually filling their tummies with low-calorie nibbles such as carrots and cucumber, they avoid hunger but fail to satisfy their appetites. The more they nibble on "slimming" snacks, the more they stimulate their taste buds and increase their appetites, and the more they need to eat. Because they never satisfy their appetites, they never feel full, even after a large meal. Their hunger-satiety mechanisms fail to work and their dieting minds take over, preventing them from feeling hungry and, consequently, from losing weight.

Constantly overeating and drinking without experiencing hunger or satiety is the first cause of obesity.

The Mood-To-Eat Cycle

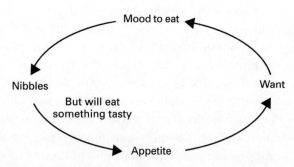

The mood-to-eat cycle

Food is a great comforter. Newborn babies suckle not only when they are hungry; many, given the chance, will continue to suckle long after they are satiated with milk, just because it soothes and comforts them. Not for nothing are babies' pacifiers commonly called comforters in the UK—love them or loathe them, they do seem to have a miraculous effect on some howling babies.

The association between food and comfort does not disappear with maturity, and many people—both slim and overweight—eat for comfort. Unlike the slimmies, though, overweight people often cannot stop once they start and they do not compensate for having overeaten. Instead, they get into the mood to eat. If your thoughts turn to food when you are bored, tired, emotionally upset, or stressed, you are a comfort eater and liable to get caught in the mood-to-eat cycle, particularly if you have sensual taste buds and a high food libido. Food lovers whose work, lifestyles, or busy social lives involve eating or drinking are also prone to falling into this cycle, as is anyone who really enjoys eating, and cannot resist tasty snacks in between meals, or trying out new tastes.

Our taste buds are quickly aroused by the sight and smell of food, but for many people the mere thought of food—and the thought of food often pops into the heads of food lovers—is enough to make you feel like eating, either nibbling or snacking, even though you are not hungry. Subconsciously you ask yourself "What shall I eat?" and soon you are off in search of a little something that might suit your fancy—that is, if it is not in your immediate vicinity and already in your mouth! One mouthful and your taste buds are triggered. Now firmly in the mood to eat, you cannot stop. Instead of simply nibbling, more often than not you have to carry on eating enough to reach food satisfaction or, beyond, to food orgasm.

In creating the mood to eat, you do not allow yourself to experience hunger and so you fail to achieve the hunger cycle.

The hunger-satiety mechanism does not prevent you from overeating because you ignore it or because, as a highly sensitive mechanism, it has been overridden and rendered useless by the overloading of your body with too much to eat and drink.

The Obsessive-Compulsive Guilt Cycle

Trying to lose weight by dieting all too frequently leads to the obsessive-compulsive guilt cycle, or guilt cycle for short (*see page 40*).

Fat People Are Not Greedy

It is the above three cycles, and their intermingling, which cause people to put on weight and become obese. When you are caught in one or more of these cycles, you have lost the natural ability to control and regulate the amount of food you eat, and the HSM, the feedback mechanism that stops you from overeating and drinking, has fallen into disuse.

Slimmies often feast more regularly than fatties because they are actually *in control* of their eating and drinking behavior. But they plan their feasts and prepare for dining out, missing or eating lightly at the meal before in anticipation, and then eating to their heart's content when the occasion arises or when they fancy a really over-the-top meal. Fatties, on the other hand, are often obsessive dieters who, once they taste forbidden or indulgent food, feel guilty and then binge compulsively. Fat people are not greedy. Most are *out of control* and so they find it impossible to lose weight.

74

What Sort of Fatty— or Slimmie—Are You?

I classify people as slimmies and fatties, the slimmies being those who look and feel slim, and are seldom seven pounds above their correct weight (the weight they look and feel good). Fatties are those who look and feel fat, and are often seven pounds or more over their correct weight. I choose seven pounds of excess weight as the dividing line between slimmies and fatties because most people begin to look plump when they go more than seven pounds above their optimum weight, and because dieters with a fat mind feel fat and bloated when they gain this much weight, aggravating guilt, and often setting in motion the whole cycle of yoyo dieting, alternately starving and bingeing.

Active Slimmies

You enjoy eating and drinking, and may well be a serious foodie, but you are in control, and able to stop. You realize that overeating and drinking make you put on weight and that alternating between being hungry and appropriately full is the body's natural rhythm. You compensate by eating less whenever you overeat. The aim of eating orgasmically is to teach active fatties to be active slimmies.

Passive Slimmies

You have been brought up or conditioned to eat normally and tend to eat regular amounts—often of the same foods—at regular times. You seldom nibble or eat between meals. You are not food mad and hunger is your signal for eating, as is fullness for stopping. On the rare occasions that you overdo it you compensate, subconsciously, by eating and drinking less at the next mealtime. Fatties envy you because they believe that you can eat whatever you please and stay slim.

Active Fatties

You eat whatever you fancy, whenever you feel the urge to do so—in fact your eating and drinking behavior often mirrors the rest of your behavior. You have highly sensual taste buds and cannot resist the indulgent foods you love. You can lose weight when you feel like it, but the discipline involved does not suit you. You are attracted to faddy diets and are likely to have developed the dieting mentality and become a compulsive eater. You are probably a victim of both the guilt cycle and the mood-to-eat cycle, and frequently fail to experience the hunger cycle. Your weight is likely to swing according to your current state of mind, and you are likely to end up even fatter unless you stop dieting.

Passive Fatties

You have most likely been brought up according to the rule that you should eat everything up—even when you are no longer hungry and no longer want to eat. ("What about all the starving children in…?") You probably assume that the large portions you are accustomed to are quite normal, eating them at regular intervals regardless of hunger. (Compensating for a large meal by undereating at the next has never occurred to you.) When you were young, you were very likely given candy or chocolates as a reward for good behavior and to comfort you when you were down. Either way, the end result is that you habitually overeat, even though you do not necessarily have a high food libido, and you rarely if ever experience the hunger cycle. You probably comfort-eat, and the more you eat the more you stimulate your taste buds, particularly if they are quite lively, leading to the mood to eat and an ever-increasing capacity for food and drink.

Passive fatties who diet and who are not obsessive, and whose food libidos are low to average, are the success stories of all slimming clubs because their eating behavior is easily conditioned. Once given a regime to follow they will automatically stick to it. Passive fatties with an obsessive personality who try to lose weight by dieting—and most dieters are a little obsessive—will acquire food obsession and the dieting mentality, become caught in the guilt cycle, and become fatter over time.

Whatever the reasons that you put on weight, if you stop dieting and acquire the art of eating you will lose weight because you will reactivate the hunger-satiety mechanism. You will relearn to enjoy food—*all* foods, including those you have previously regarded with suspicion as "forbidden" or "unhealthy" when you were on the dieting treadmill—without any guilt, at the same time as you reduce your eating capacity and get into shape.

5

Enter the Diet-Free Zone: Discover the Principles of Eating Orgasmically and Learn to Eat Like a Slimmie

If you are reading this book then you are probably not as slim as you would like to be or maybe you are worried that you will not stay slim, and are searching for a way to keep flab away for good. If you have tried dieting, you probably found that when you stopped and returned to your usual eating pattern all the weight you lost piled back on again, and more into the bargain. Is there a genuine solution? Can food lovers really lose weight and stay in shape?

Yes, by entering the diet-free zone and learning the art of eating orgasmically, not addictively!

In this chapter you will learn the basic tools of eating orgasmically and begin to disengage yourself from patterns or cycles of eating behavior which have contributed to your weight gain. Eating orgasmically is based on the eating behavior of naturally slim people, and following the guidelines in the rest of the book will train you into slim eating habits for life. The fundamental principles of eating orgasmically are *rhythm* and *compensation,* which together put you in *control.* Losing weight involves reducing the amount you eat and your eating capacity. It is achieved by controlling your appetite and your eating habits, but never by using your willpower to starve, which makes you lose control and is always followed by the inevitable binge. When you are in control, you can overeat and experience food orgasm whenever you want to, but you will do so intentionally, enjoying your food without guilt. By employing the art of compensation you will be able to overeat without gaining weight because you will have established an eating rhythm suited to your lifestyle.

To begin with, you will need to practice eating orgasmically consciously, following the quick or gentle version of the basic eating rhythm (*see Chapter 7*), which is designed to retrain your eating habits and reduce your eating capacity, and using the three mental exercises (*see page 85*) to overcome your dieting mind. But before long you will have adapted the art of eating to meet your own needs and rhythms, and learned the art of compensation. Then eating orgasmically will become second nature.

Feeling the Rhythm—Getting in Tune with Your Body

As I explained in the last chapter, the natural rhythm of the body is to be hungry...full...hungry...full. People who listen to their bodies, eating in response to hunger signals and stopping when satisfied, normally get hungry three or maybe four times a day and are sensitive to their nutritional needs. The most common rhythm is to eat three meals a day, evenly spaced if possible: breakfast, lunch, and dinner. One of these—lunch or dinner—is usually the main meal, the other two being light meals, with the occasional food, such as a cookie, a bar of chocolate, or a piece of fruit, in between. For some personalities and lifestyles this rhythm is unfeasible, however, which is why it is important to establish your own rhythm, perfectly in tune with your needs and tastes. All eating rhythms should, of course, consist of a balanced and healthy diet, and all should involve experiencing hunger for a little while in between meals.

A slimming rhythm is any rhythm which reduces your weekly intake of food, and means being hungry, at any rate to begin with, for more of the time than a rhythm designed just to maintain your weight and stay in shape. If you do not get hungry, you will not lose weight. Not only that, but you will never satisfy your body's needs, either, if you do not listen or respond to its signals of satiety, and do not wait for hunger signals before eating. If your hunger-satiety mechanism has fallen out of use, practicing the mental exercises and following the basic rhythm will soon reactivate it as you learn to experience and accept the feeling of hunger. In the process you will also reduce your eating capacity, as your stomach adjusts to and expects less food, and take control.

A word of warning: letting yourself get *too* hungry is as fatal to losing weight as never getting hungry in the first place. When you try to starve away the excess pounds, ignoring clear hunger signals and the pressing demands of your body to be fed, you end up losing control. When you eventually eat, you go mad and wolf down everything in sight, consuming far more in one uncontrollable binge than you would have done had you eaten while you were hungry, but still in control.

The whole rationale of a slimming rhythm is to exploit your hunger without letting it go out of control.

Slimming rhythms, like other eating rhythms, need to be flexible enough to accommodate all the requirements of your lifestyle, whether for social eating like dinner parties, or for corporate entertaining or special occasions, as well as your regular routine. They should also suit your personality and health. Because I have an obsessive personality and was an active fattie, I was desperate to lose weight fast—25 to 42 pounds in two or three months—so I used the quickest possible rhythm suited to my lifestyle. If you are in less of a hurry to lose weight, follow a slower, more gentle rhythm, which will still result in a weight loss of one to three pounds a week.

To accommodate the different rates at which my clients wish to lose weight, I have devised two versions of the basic rhythm, quick and gentle, which are explained in detail in Chapter 7. But the basic rhythm is just the beginning of your new approach to food. Once you have got the hang of it, you can ring the changes. Eating rhythms are based on weekly and sometimes even monthly food intake, rather than being geared purely to what you eat in a day. This allows for variations from one day to the next. Suppose, for example, that you will be eating a lot over the weekend for social or family reasons, and are going out for a meal on Thursday night. Then, if you want to lose weight, you can simply adopt a slimming rhythm for that week of eating less on Monday and Tuesday, normally on Wednesday, enjoying whatever you want when you go out on Thursday, having eaten lightly at breakfast and lunch, and then less again on Friday in anticipation of the weekend.

Chapter 7 is devoted to the basic rhythm, which most of my clients start off with in one or other of its forms, what to expect on a week-by-week basis, and how to cope with unlearning old eating patterns. Chapter 8 includes a variety of different weekly rhythms designed to fit different lifestyles. All the rhythms can be used as set out in this book or adapted to your own lifestyle. The name of the game is to find your *own* rhythm.

Taking Control

Most diets last as long as the dieter's will to abstain from foods they need, love, or crave holds out. Dieters are usually strong-willed, using their strength of purpose to impose on themselves strict regimes which deprive them of any food satisfaction, conflict with their normal way of life, go against the natural flow of their bodies and go out of control. When they give in to temptation—which they inevitably do—they feel weak-willed, depressed, and are liable to give up their diets, returning to their original eating habits. Dieters who are strongly motivated—say by a special forthcoming event like a wedding or the prospect of a vacation in the sun, lazing around in a swimsuit or bikini—often succeed in losing a lot of weight using willpower to abstain temporarily. But once the event is over, the vacation has arrived, then the diet is over. They relax their willpower and go berserk. Once they taste the forbidden foods they have denied themselves, many get caught up in a great tidal wave of overeating, unable to stop; others simply return to eating "normally" again, in other words to their old, fat, eating habits. Either way, the weight piles on again. They are either *on* a diet or *off* a diet, but never eating normally.

Using willpower to resist your body's basic requirement for regular injections of fuel—a sufficient quantity of the right kinds of foods to satisfy its needs at least two or three times daily—is not the way to achieve permanent weight loss. At best it achieves short-term results. More often it is the fast route to uncontrolled, erratic eating and the dieting mentality.

Controlling the food you eat, on the other hand, allows you to decide what you want, when you want it, and to enjoy eating it, knowing you will be able to stop when you wish. Control means working with your body, not against it, adopting a pattern of eating that fits in with your lifestyle and allows you the foods that you enjoy, and enough of them to feel satisfied.

When you have satisfied your appetite as well as your body's nutritional requirements, it is relatively easy to control your eating behavior until the next mealtime, especially in comparison to the strength of will needed to resist snacks when you are genuinely very hungry.

When you take control, steeling your will in a vain attempt to defeat the twin demons of hunger and food cravings becomes a thing of the past. When you feel the urge to nibble or eat, you simply ask yourself whether you really want two, three, four, five or however many bars of chocolate, bags of chips or whatever to achieve food satisfaction or food orgasm. If you are not sure, or you know you do not really want to eat—you are just bored, tired or emotional, then wait a few moments (*see diagram page 92*). The urge might pass. If you really do want to eat, go ahead and enjoy it without panicking, and without feeling guilty. But make sure you compensate later!

The Art of Compensation

Compensating for over- or undereating is simple, natural and obvious, and is practiced by all the "lucky" people who manage to stay slim in spite of frequently tucking in with great gusto to enormous lunches and dinners. When such people overeat, they redress the balance later, either instinctively because they are sensitive to their bodies' needs, or by consciously eating less the next day or at the next meal.

The art of compensation is essential to the art of eating, whether you wish to lose weight or simply maintain your weight. The art of compensation is the art of maintaining a balance, which keeps or brings you back into shape.

Keeping your weight in balance is a bit like keeping your bank account in balance. When you spend too much money, you go into overdraft. You now have a loan from the bank and will have to pay back the debt. The more you borrow from the bank, the harder it becomes to repay the loan, and the higher the interest on the loan becomes, increasing the amount you owe yet more. It is better to pay off your overdraft regularly, before it gets out of hand and becomes a large loan. In a similar way, when you eat too much, you are taking out a "loan" of fat which will make you put on weight if you do not repay it. The more you eat without paying back, the greater your fat deposit becomes, and the harder to shift.

Like a lot of people, I get an enormous kick out of spending, eating, and drinking. Paying back is not the same kind of fun, admittedly, but it can be curiously satisfying, and certainly need not mean deprivation. Personally I enjoy enormously the splurges that I have "earned"—but when I constantly overate I rarely enjoyed it that much. Paying back your loan and keeping the bank manager happy is much more conducive to a stress-free life without complications than getting into more and more debt. That means spending, or eating and drinking less, until you are back in balance.

Although the principle of compensating is quite straightforward and obvious, it is a concept which eludes and is even rejected by many dieters and fatties. The dieting mind panics at the mere sight of a decent meal, so when you eat well, say at a dinner party, instead of enjoying it you feel guilty. At the same time your taste buds, often deprived of "forbidden" foods, are awakened by delicious tastes and raring to go. This, in combination with your conflicting emotions about food, can often set you off on further eating. So, unlike the natural slimmie who compensates after overeating and drinking by missing the next meal or eating lightly, you go and eat more. The three mental exercises (*see opposite*) are designed to combat this.

Train Your Mind to Control Your Body with the Three Mental Exercises

The functions of our bodies and minds, though inextricably connected, are very different. The body is our physical apparatus, and to function optimally it needs food and drink at regular intervals, according to the hungry...full...hungry...full rhythm. The mind is the faculty which enables us to think, feel, and will. Ideally these three functions, thought (T), feeling or fancy (F), and willpower (W) are in balance:

T
F
W

As a dieter, however, you have very strong willpower as you have been training your will to abstain from eating "forbidden" foods that your body needs and your mind desires. The picture in your case is more like this:

T
F
W

Dieters who wish to suppress their love of food have to exert even more willpower, distorting the mind's equilibrium even further:

T
F
W

In food phobics and obsessive dieters who succeed in killing off their desire or fancy for food, while constantly thinking about food and their weight, the picture looks like this:

T
F
W

While the minds of those who are out of shape because they constantly give in to their fancy for food look like this:

T
F
W

The minds of fatties who are strong-willed and determined to eat as much of whatever they fancy whenever they fancy have the following shape:

T
F
W

The three mental exercises will overcome the imbalance between the functions of thought, feeling, and willpower and train your mind to listen to your body so that sometimes you *think* about food but you may not fancy or want it.

T
F
W

Other times you may not think about food but you *fancy* something to eat,

T

F

W

Or you may neither think about nor fancy food, but you *want* something to eat,

T

F

W

But when you *think* about food, you *fancy* it and *want* it, then you *eat orgasmically.*

T
F
W

Practicing the three mental exercises below trains your mind to follow the natural flow of the body and helps to balance the faculties of thought, feeling, and will. This balance is a prerequisite of eating orgasmically, which involves making a rational decision about the food you love, and then going for it if that is what you wish to do, and enjoying it.

Exercise 1

Always say to yourself after eating: "I really enjoyed that!"
Never say to yourself: "I wish I had not eaten that."

Whenever you say to yourself mentally after eating—whether nibbling, bingeing, or simply having a good meal—that you wish you had not, you are reinforcing the dieting mentality and destroying your pleasure in food. Instead, convince yourself that you really enjoyed it, and that you were really satisfied by it, mentally repeating this to yourself whenever you eat. When your dieting mindset tries to sabotage the exercise, as it will to begin with, telling you that you really *do* wish you had not eaten, do not worry. Just allow it to rattle on, without paying too much attention and counteracting it with the more positive message that you really enjoyed your food. Practicing this whenever you eat goes a long way toward overcoming the guilt that does so much damage, and which has no place in the art of eating.

Exercise 2

When you feel hungry between meals remember:
Hunger is losing weight.

To help you grow accustomed to the full...hungry...full...hungry...eating rhythm, and the feeling of being hungry if you are unused to it, you need to realize and remember the importance of hunger. When you are hungry, your stomach is empty and so your body has to draw on its reserves of fat for energy. The result is that you lose weight.

By allowing yourself to be hungry for a while before your next meal, but without skipping a meal, which can lead to overeating, you get back in touch with your body, reactivating the hungersatiety mechanism. When you become sensitive to your body's signals, you will naturally understand what foods your body needs and when.

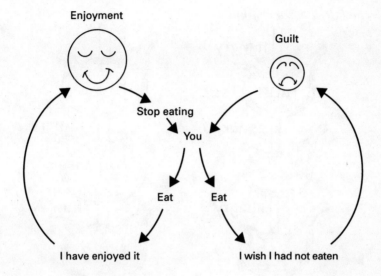

Eating orgasmically

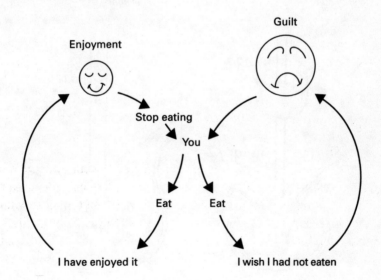

Dieting

The full–hungry rhythm

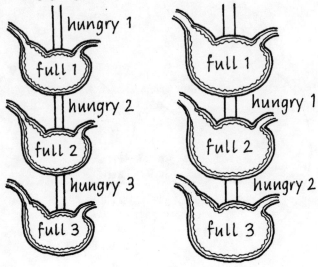

hungry 1

full 1

hungry 2

full 2

hungry 3

full 3

To stay slim

full 1

hungry 1

full 2

hungry 2

full 3

To put on weight

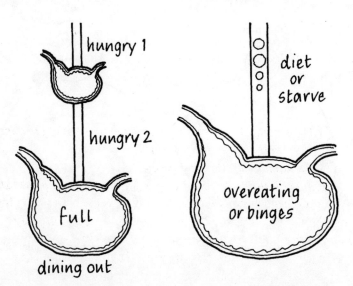

hungry 1

hungry 2

full

dining out

To overeat knowingly and stay slim

diet
or
starve

overeating
or binges

To overeat knowingly and binge

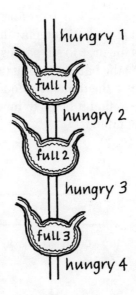

hungry 1

full 1

hungry 2

full 2

hungry 3

full 3

hungry 4

To lose weight

By controlling your appetite and experiencing hunger for a while before eating you will also reduce your eating capacity, as your stomach will shrink and feel full with less food.

Exercise 3

Control comfort eating and the mood to eat by asking yourself: "Do I really want it?"

If yes, then go ahead and enjoy it.

If you are not sure, wait and see how you feel a bit later.
When the urge to eat takes hold of you, yet it is not time for a meal, or if you cannot stop eating even though you know you have really had enough, think about whether you are really hungry, or really want to eat more. If you are, then indulge yourself with whatever it is you want, enjoy it, and do not feel guilty. If you are not sure, postpone it for a few moments

or minutes. Count slowly to 10 or, better still, get out of the kitchen. The heat is too hot! You may find that by waiting even for a few seconds the urge to eat passes away. The initial delay is the key to losing the habit of eating the moment you feel like it or simply because the thought of food has popped into your head. You may also find it helps to buy only what you need— out of sight, out of mind.

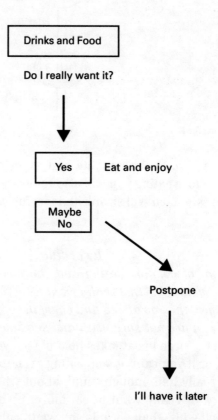

Postponing eating

This exercise helps you learn how to stop eating and drinking when you have had enough, in other words how to stop—and prevent—the mood-to-eat cycle. It teaches you to take control by reminding you to think about what your body really needs and wants, so you make choices on that basis rather than obeying momentary whims. By postponing food, however briefly, when you are in the mood to eat, you will not only lose weight but you will stop using food as an emotional outlet and may well find more constructive ways to deal with life's rich smorgasbord of emotions, stress, boredom, and other ups and downs.

By consciously practicing these three mental exercises, you will subconsciously begin to think like a naturally slim person. You will transform your fat or dieting mindset into a thin one. When you combine thinking like a thin person with eating like a thin person, which you will find out about in the next two chapters, you will lose weight and you will lose it for good.

6

The Art of Compensation and the "Rules" of the Game

Like all the other skills we acquire throughout our lives—
whether it is the art of conversation or the art of driving a car
—the arts of eating and compensation have to be consciously
learned and practiced. But just like talking and driving, with
time they become second nature, and you rarely have to consciously think about what, when, and how you are going to
eat. As you become sensitized to your body's signals and
needs for food, you will instinctively tune in to the eating
rhythm best suited to you and automatically compensate for
a large meal by eating less at the next meal. But to begin
with, I have found the simple expedient of using the rims of a
plate an excellent way to explain and teach the practical art
of compensation.

The Art of Compensation: Using Your Plates to Pay Back Your Fat Loan

To learn the skill and art of compensation, and to control the amount you eat, you need nothing more than the plates you eat on. What could be simpler? The size of your plate already controls the amount you eat, so long as you do not go back for second and third helpings! But you can take this further by dividing the plate up into three "rims."

The idea of the plate began many years ago in Vienna, where I was staying with a most delightful family who believed in eating very, very well. The lady of the house was an excellent cook who turned every meal into a Viennese feast. Deciding what to eat was my main problem. Having just lost 35 lb, and with another seven pounds to lose, I panicked at the mere sight of all the richly delicious Austrian savories and cakes: the famous Sachertorte, the original recipe of which is a closely guarded secret of the Hotel Sacher, dripping with dark, glistening chocolate and served with a huge dollop of whipped cream; Linzertorte full of raspberries latticed with melt-in-the-mouth hazelnut pastry; steaming cups of hot chocolate; Wiener Schnitzel, the classic Austrian way to serve veal, with sauté potatoes...There seemed little hope of staying slim!

But I established a two-meal-a-day eating rhythm, with nothing in between. Missing breakfast stopped me thinking about food, and eating two good meals a day stopped me "picking." I felt in control, and with all these rich new tastes I recaptured the magic of good food and drink. But how was I going to stay slim, let alone lose weight, with all this exquisite food to tempt my taste buds?

My *plate*, of course. Staring at my plate, I heard my mother's voice insisting that the Chinese stay slim without dieting, and that they do so by not eating "beyond the plate" every day. It is not the kind of food you eat, but the amount of it that you eat, that makes you fat. From that moment onwards I ate twice each day within the normal rim of the plate, and went into an imaginary inner rim whenever I overate. By using the plate in this way I had also, by accident, discovered a way to reduce my eating and drinking capacity.

By going in and out of the rims like this, I ate orgasmically and still lost five pounds during my three-week stay in Vienna. Not only was it a most wonderful holiday but I was back in shape at last and back in control. I returned to England looking and feeling good. That was nearly 40 years ago, and since then I have never put on more than two or three pounds, which I have quickly lost again!

The Normal, Inner, and Outer Rims

To teach the art and skill of compensation, I give all the new clients that I see in my clinics a special plate with three rims— outer, normal and inner:

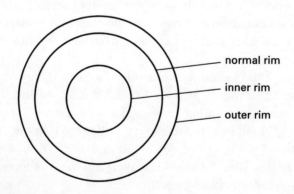

normal rim

inner rim

outer rim

The special plate

This is simply a traditional plate with a raised edge or rim. The outer rim or edge of the plate is just over 10 inches in diameter. The normal rim, marked by forget-me-not motif in the form of a circle, is the boundary between the raised rim and the flat surface of the plate, and is six-and-a-half or seven inches in diameter. Within this is a second circular forget-me-not motif—the inner rim—which is four inches in diameter.

Although this specially designed plate is a useful tool, to learn the art of compensation using the rims method you can use any traditional plate with a normal rim, which gives a guide to a normal helping. The inner rim can simply be an imaginary rim about the size of a large potato or apple, or a cream bun.

To stay slim our bodies normally require three meals a day, each meal being within the normal rim. If you overeat and go beyond the rim, then you should pay back by eating within the inner rim at the next meal or the next day. To lose weight you will need to eat less—say the amount of two meals a day within the normal rim, which you can eat as two meals within the inner rim and one meal within the normal rim. By adopting such a rhythm you will be paying back one plate (normal rim) a day, but anything less than three normal rims a day and you will lose excess weight.

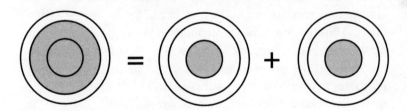

Normal rim = 2 inner rims

If you nibble and/or binge beyond the rim, do not panic and do not feel guilty. Tell yourself you have enjoyed it, and pay back with two inner rims the next day. Likewise, if you are at a party or you are dining out and in the mood to eat, then do not limit yourself—go for food orgasm! After all, most of us, and certainly most active slimmies, overeat when we go out or when we just happen to feel like it. Eat all you want and enjoy it, but remember to compensate by eating within the inner rim at the previous meal and/or at the next.

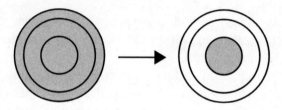

Eating orgasmically, then paying back with an inner rim

Counting Your Foods

As well as controlling the amount you eat by using the rims of your plates, you can count the number of foods you eat at each meal. Although counting your foods has no place in the ultimate scheme of things, when you will be in shape and have so internalized the art of eating that it will be instinctive, it is a useful technique to add to your repertoire of fatbusting equipment, especially if you want to lose weight fast.

One of the most effective ways of controlling your appetite is to restrict the number of different foods you eat, which is why diets which limit you to one or two kinds of foods, such as grapefruit or eggs, can be very effective for short-term weight loss, even though they are nutritionally unsound. There is a limit to the number of soft or hard boiled eggs you can eat at a sitting, or even in a day! Our taste buds thrive on variety, which stimulates them and increases our appetites, but they quickly become satiated with a single food—even if it is one you adore. This is why you can still, miraculously, make room for pudding even when you are so full after your main course that you cannot eat another mouthful of it.

American eating habits have undergone a revolution in the last two decades, but the quintessential American meal, well balanced nutritionally, remains the traditional plate of meat and two veg. So long as your serving is within the normal rim, this counts as three foods, as sauces and gravy are not counted as foods in this system. When you eat three meals of three foods a day, all within the normal rim, you will maintain your weight and stay in shape. If you cut down from nine to six, seven or eight foods a day, you will lose weight.

Examples

One Food

- **One fruit**: from a small plum to a large banana, apple, orange, half grapefruit, etc.
  one tomato, pepper, avocado, etc.
  one heaped tablespoon of grapes, berries, etc.
  one slice of pineapple, melon, watermelon, etc.
- **One heaped serving spoon of any vegetables**: any cooked vegetables, salad, baked beans, bean salad, coleslaw, stir fry, potatoes, etc.
- **One heaped serving spoon of any cereal**: corn flakes, uncooked oats, rice, noodles, pasta, etc.

- **One large ladle of**: soup, stew, casserole, chilli con carne,
- **One**: egg, sausage, slice of bacon
  slice of unbuttered bread or toast, roll
  cookie bun, slice of plain or fruit cake, muffin, scone,
  doughnut, 2½ oz / 65g bar of chocolate
  scoop of ice cream, serving spoon of fruit salad, 2½ oz
  (65 g) bar of plain or milk chocolate
- **4 – 5 oz of**: any meat, fish, seafood, chicken, duck, cheese

Two Foods

- **Pies, the size of the inner rim or within it**:
  apple or any sweet pie, rhubarb crumble, etc.
  a large bar (4 oz/100 g) of chocolate with raisins or nuts
  two bars of chocolate (2½ oz/65 g) without nuts or raisins
- **One portion**: lasagne, pizza, rice, risotto, paella, noodles,
  pasta (with any kind of sauce, including fish, meat or
  vegetable sauce)
- **One large**: baked potato
  slice of bread or toast with butter or margarine or two
  slices unbuttered
  kingsize bar of chocolate with nuts, raisins or biscuit (e.g.
  a KitKat) or two bars of milk or plain chocolate
  120 g bar cookie with nuts and chocolate, cake with icing,
  slice of plain cake with chocolate or cream filling

Three Foods

one giant scone with fruit jelly and cream cheese
one slice of bread or toast with butter and fruit jelly or
marmalade, three slices without butter or fruit jelly
one sandwich with 4 oz of filling but no butter
one hamburger or vegeburger
one large baked potato with any filling

one pizza or pie filling the normal rim
one large bar of chocolate to fill the normal rim, two
kingsize bars or three 2½ oz/65 g bars milk or plain
chocolate

Four Foods

a normal sandwich with butter and 4 oz of filling

Summer Fruits and Whipped Cream; Fruit Compôtes

A cereal bowl or plateful of any soft fruit—strawberries, raspberries, red or blackcurrants—with or without cream and
sugar is a meal, or three foods. Similarly a large bowl of fruit
compôte or fruit salad—apricots, plums, pears, peaches,
prunes, and so on, whether in wine or liquor, with or without
whipped cream and sugar, is a meal or three foods.

Alternatively you can have a serving spoonful as one food,
or a small bowl as two foods.

Soups

A large bowl of thick or creamy soup with vegetables, potatoes, corn, chicken, etc., or fish soups or stews such as the
French *bouillabaisse* with fish and shellfish, is a meal.

A cup of thick soup counts as one food, whereas a cup of
thin soup—consommé or clear chicken soup—counts as a
drink.

*When you socialize and eat orgasmically you do not count
food. You eat and drink to your heart's content, without
restraint, until your taste buds are satiated and your
appetite is fulfilled. Aim to eat orgasmically once or twice a
week while you are losing weight.*

The list of foods above may surprise you, especially if you are used to thinking in terms of calories and "forbidden" foods. But counting foods has *nothing* whatever to do with counting calories—and it is much simpler! Have you ever seen a calorie? Or tried counting calories? Calories are scientific measurements of energy best left to scientists with the right technology to calculate them. Recent press reports have claimed that the calorie content specified on the packaging of foods sold in supermarkets is often quite inaccurate, and the armchair calculations of dieters are unlikely to fare any better. Calorie counting is not a reliable or practical way to control your food intake.

Counting foods, on the other hand, helps to change your attitude toward food, opposing your dieting mentality, and modifying your eating and drinking behavior. As you can see from the table above, a large or small lettuce leaf or banana, a baked potato and a bar of chocolate, are all examples of one food. If you were restricted to six or eight foods a day, which foods would you choose? People with a normal, healthy attitude to food would choose a balanced mix of filling foods, such as a banana, muffin, pasta, baked potato or a beef burrito, plus some protein—a portion of fish, meat, eggs, or cheese, and maybe a bar of chocolate, a scoop of ice cream, or a slice of cake. Not so the dieter, who would avoid foods such as the burrito and ice cream, because they have too many calories, choosing instead lettuce leaves, fruit, pasta with a low-fat sauce, and suchlike. But although lettuce, vegetables, and fruit have a great reputation amongst slimmers, who often try to acquire a taste for them, if they do not particularly like them by nature, the truth is that lettuce is too low in calories and insufficiently dense to be able to fill your stomach—it just does not fill you up, and leaves you unsatisfied. Similarly with fruit and vegetables, which are mainly sugar and starch and lack the sustaining power that really counts.

This is why dieters nibble, unable to control their eating behavior. They do not eat enough filling foods to meet the minimum energy requirements of their bodies, which react by rebelling and propelling the dieter into an unscheduled and uncontrolled snacking session or binge.

Food for Thought: A Balanced Diet

A little of what you fancy—pâté de fois gras, death-by-chocolate cake, Chinese takeout, Irish coffee brimming with Irish whiskey and heavy cream—does you good, so long as you do not feel guilty about it. So eat, drink, and be merry, but maintain your self-control. The secret of slimming is to control how much, how often, and what you eat, and to maintain a balance. My purpose is to help you think more about *how much* and *how often* you eat, but I firmly believe that *what* you eat is up to you. There are no fattening foods, nor any slimming foods that make you lose weight. Believing in them only reinforces the dieting mentality.

It is true, though, that the human body needs a balanced combination of protein, fats, carbohydrates, vitamins, and minerals to function properly. It is perfectly possible to eat nothing but "health" foods—organic fruit, vegetables, cereals, and so on—yet have a poor diet, because you are not eating a nutritional balance of food. Similarly you can have an overall healthy, balanced diet which includes a certain amount of sugar and chocolate. Balance is the key. When you are in tune with your body, your appetite and taste buds will automatically guide you in your choice of foods so that your nutritional requirements are filled, much as you will automatically adjust your food intake to match your energy requirements (*see Metabolism, page 62*). However, if you are unsure of your nutritional needs, make sure you eat a variety of foods and that you daily eat foods from each of the columns in the table below. As you will see, the columns overlap. Milk, for example, is a complete food containing protein, carbohydrate, fats, vitamins, and minerals—the natural food of all infants, containing all their requirements until they are weaned. However, it is not the natural food of adults, and you will not lose weight if you punctuate the intervals between meals with rich, milky drinks!

The Foods Your Body Needs

Proteins	Fats	Carbohydrates	Vitamins	Minerals
meat	oils, e.g., olive,	potatoes	salads	vegetables,
fish	sunflower	cereals	vegetables	e.g., carrots,
poultry	butter	pasta and rice	fruit	broccoli
peas, beans,	margarine	bread and	beans and	beans and
and lentils	cheese	cakes	lentils	lentils
milk	meat	salads and	milk	milk
	oily fish	fruit		
	milk	vegetables		
		milk		

Some kinds of foods fill you and satisfy your appetite more than others. These *filler foods* include potatoes, rice, bread, baked beans, pasta and other fillings foods. On the other hand, some foods just make you want to eat more. They stimulate your taste buds and are liable to put you in the mood to eat. *Indulgent foods* are things like crisps, salted roasted nuts and peanuts, roast potatoes and chips, melted cheese on baked potatoes, curry, spare ribs with chilli sauce, chocolates, nuts, cookies, cakes, and other sweet foods. Foods like these can overstimulate your taste buds and trigger you into carrying on eating until you experience food orgasm. If they do, learn which are your trigger foods and limit them to twice a week while you are trying to lose weight. Only have them in the house when you intend to eat them!

Slimming Strategies

Although in reality there are no "rules" about eating orgasmically, I have found that many of my clients like to establish a few ground rules, especially in the early stages of getting accustomed to a slimming rhythm and learning how to adapt it. The following guidelines will help you to adopt slim eating habits and a new attitude to losing weight while you are slimming. They are not necessary for staying slim.

1. Silence is Golden

If you do not tell anyone that you are slimming, then no one will try to dissuade you or persuade you to eat and drink. Even the best of friends can feel threatened if you lose weight and they do not, or if they are used to being the slim one, and you the fattie. Slim people rarely admit to cutting down—they just allow the results to speak for themselves. In any case they only have a few pounds to lose because they always pay back before matters get out of hand. So, do not turn down food you are offered on the grounds that you are slimming. Decline politely if you do not want to eat it. If you are dining out, enjoy yourself and eat orgasmically, and pay back later. When you look and feel good, you have reached your correct weight— then you can explain that you have discovered the art of eating like a naturally thin person!

2. Weigh Yourself Weekly

Weigh yourself when you begin your slimming rhythm, and work out your body mass index (BMI) (*see page 53*). If it is over 25, aim for a BMI of 25 before slimming down to your correct weight and shape. If it is 25 or under, follow a slimming rhythm until you are within the BMI/weight range corresponding to your body type (*see page 54*) and have become your ideal shape. Weigh yourself weekly, not daily. Weight can fluctuate from day to day without any apparent bearing on what you have eaten in the day, so to avoid confusion, and obsession, step on the scales once a week only, preferably first thing in the morning and wearing the same or no clothes.

3. Sit and Eat Two, Three, or More Meals Daily. Avoid Breakfast if it Triggers You into Nibbling All Day!

Sit down and eat two or three meals daily, to the amount of anything less than three normal rims or nine foods a day, and avoid nibbling in between. If work or your lifestyle dictates that you should eat more often, or if you simply prefer to, then you can spread this amount to four, five, or six small meals (of one or two foods) a day. Most of my clients eat two or three meals a day, depending on whether or not eating breakfast tends to set them off nibbling for the rest of the day. Obsessive dieters and comfort eaters often find that breakfast is a trigger meal for them, resulting in more eating during the rest of the day. This makes them feel guilty, setting in motion the vicious guilt cycle. Avoid breakfast and eat an early lunch if breakfast is your downfall. Active fatties and food lovers with highly active taste buds will also be triggered into eating all day if they eat as soon as they get up. They should have a late breakfast—two or three hours after they get up, or an early lunch.

Try not to nibble in between meals—you will not need to if you have satisfied your appetite. If you do, pay back as soon as possible, preferably at the next mealtime, by eating within the inner rim or by eating one food less. If you want to stop nibbling, but feel out of control, eat some filling food, such as a large baked potato or a bowl of pasta. When you have lost weight and want to nibble, you can follow the nibbling rhythm —but until you are slim and fully in control, it is better to limit or curb the habit.

Space your meals evenly if possible and do not go longer than a maximum of six waking hours in a day without food. Remember: you will lose control if you become too hungry or overeat too frequently.

4. Limit the Amount You Eat.
Eat Within the Normal Rim

Eat the amount of two normal rims or two normal rims and one inner rim daily (except on the occasions you go out and eat beyond the rim). You are paying back one, or half, a plate daily. Whenever you overeat, make sure you compensate.

5. Limit the Amount You Drink

Limit the amount you drink to approximately three and a half pints of fluid or about seven drinks daily, including water, tea, coffee, milk (one pint a week, preferably semi-skimmed). Remember that eating orgasmically represents a new way of thinking – even sweet drinks contain some sort of sugar. If you are thirsty then drink extra plain water.

Halve the amount of alcohol and fruit juice that you drink. Avoid or drink very few soft drinks, fizzy drinks, diet, or low-calorie drinks. These are trigger drinks for many people, which will set you off nibbling or bingeing. You cannot afford them too often when you are trying to lose weight.

6. Start a Food Diary

Write down what you eat and drink, and when you eat and drink it, in your diary. Many overweight people suffer from what I call "dieting amnesia." They either forget or block out of their minds how much they really eat. Unlike slim people, who tend to remember what and when they eat, fat people remember when they do not eat.

Getting into the habit, temporarily, of recording what and when you eat, as you eat it or as soon afterward as you can, will make you more aware of what you are eating and you will not need to worry about whether or not you have eaten more than you planned to. Use your regular diary or make photocopies of the specially designed diary page opposite. Nobody except you need see what you write in your diary, so be honest with yourself. There is no need to cheat when you can eat and drink whatever you want and however much you want, as long as you remember to compensate within the inner rim. The diary is to help you establish your slimming rhythm.

time	mon	tues	wed	thurs	fri	sat	sun
up							
bed							
start work							
finish work							
meals	time	time	time	time	time	time	time
meals	time	time	time	time	time	time	time
meals	time	time	time	time	time	time	time
drinks							

weekly weight

A food diary

7. Eat a Balanced Diet

Remember that you need to eat a balanced diet, with a good variety of foods, to ensure that all your nutritional needs are met and that you keep fit and well. Eating a balanced combination of filler foods, such as baked potatoes, pasta, and rice, and any indulgent foods that you really enjoy—roast potatoes, onion rings, pork rinds, olives, cookies or chocolate—is also important. If you do not have enough of your favorite foods you will get bored and start nibbling. If you overeat or peak on rich, saturated, fatty foods, then balance this later by eating fat-free foods or unsaturated fats, and compensating when appropriate.

8. Know Your Triggers

Eating orgasmically means enjoying as much as you want of the foods you love and crave, *knowing how to stop when you want to*. In the early stages of eating orgasmically, and when you are slimming, the sight and smell of foods you find highly orgasmic and indulgent can easily trigger you into overeating when you do not actually wish to. If you know that cheese crackers, crispy fried bacon, eclairs, or chocolate will set you off, avoid having them in the house until you feel firmly in control. On the other hand, if you decide that you cannot live a minute longer without the food that you crave, then go out and buy a packet or two of cookies or bacon, or three bars of chocolate, or whatever it is that you crave, and consume as much as you need to experience food orgasm. Pay back at the next meal or the next day!

9. You May Not Lose Weight Every Week

Circumstances such as vacations, entertaining, or just reaching a temporary plateau may mean that you are unable to lose weight every week. There is no need to worry—plateaux happen when you have been eating orgasmically for a few weeks, and if you are overeating knowingly then you can pay back as soon as convenient. Try to maintain your current weight.

10. Most Important of All, RELAX AND ENJOY YOUR FOOD. Do Not Panic if You Overeat or Binge Now and Again

There is no such thing as cheating when you eat orgasmically, because you can eat and drink as much as you like so long as you compensate—and it is always better to do so sooner rather than later. I encourage *all* my clients—and some take a lot of persuading!—to have at least one, and maybe two, orgasmic feasts a week, as you will see in the next chapter. If you binge or overdo it one day, you pay back the next. You have not blown it, and it will not stop you losing weight!

The aim of eating orgasmically is to acquire the art of eating and drinking like a slimmie, enjoying your food as you regain and retain your ideal body shape. Turn to the next chapter to get into rhythm and start losing weight now!

7

Get into Rhythm and Start Losing Weight Quickly or Gently with the Basic Rhythm

You now have a large repertoire of fat-unfriendly arts. All you need is to get into rhythm and then you can start watching your surplus stores of fat melt away and wave goodbye to flab forever. Begin with either the quick or the gentle basic rhythm, below. If you want to lose weight fast—between five and seven pounds in the first week, 14 lb in three to five weeks—then use the quick rhythm and count foods, increasing quantities slightly after the first week. Using the gentle rhythm you will lose from one up to three pounds in the first week, and 14 lbs in six or eight weeks.

Remember that the basic rhythm, quick or gentle, is only a guide. Follow it for a few weeks, adapting it if you wish, to suit you and your lifestyle, or go straight into the rhythm of your choice. If you have only about seven pounds to lose, and you do not want or need to do it overnight, you can use the control rhythm (*page 162*) if you prefer. If you want to lose it in a hurry, just before a beach vacation perhaps, then you can do it with the quick rhythm but you will put all the weight back on again unless you follow it up with the gentle or control rhythms.

The Basic Rhythm

To stay slim, your body needs three meals a day, all within the normal rim (or three meals of three foods, if you are counting foods). Anything less and you will lose weight. There are two basic rhythms. The quick rhythm allows you the amount of two normal rims a day (six foods), which can be spread over three or four meals. The gentle rhythm allows you the amount of two and a half normal rims a day (seven or eight foods). Once or twice a week you should fulfill your desire for the foods you love and crave by eating orgasmically—eating as much as you want of whatever you want without restraint, and without worry or guilt because you will be compensating either before or afterwards!

Quick Rhythm

The quick rhythm should be used for a maximum of three weeks continuously. If you use it for longer than this, your body will rebel and you will binge.

Many of my clients use the quick rhythm as their basic rhythm for the first one to three weeks, returning to it again after a break of two or more weeks. This rhythm is especially suited to active fatties, with their high food libidos and passionate taste buds. It is also indispensable for anyone who needs to lose weight fast before an important event or a vacation. I also

Example of the quick rhythm

	To stay slim	To lose weight rhythm 1	To lose weight rhythm 2
	3 meals a day	2 meals a day	3 meals a day
	Monday	**Tuesday**	**Wednesday**
Up	7 A.M.	7 A.M.	7 A.M.
Bed	10.30 P.M.	11 P.M.	10.30 P.M.
Start work	8.30 – 9 A.M.	8.30 – 9 A.M.	8.30 – 9 A.M.
Finish work	5 – 5.30 P.M.	5 – 5.30 P.M.	5 – 5.30 P.M.
On waking	2 cups of tea/coffee	2 cups of tea/coffee	2 cups of tea/coffee
Meal 1	10 – 10.30 A.M. 1 banana	10 – 10.30 A.M. 1 banana	10 – 10.30 A.M. 1 banana
Meal 2	12.30 – 1.30 P.M. pasta with any sauce	12.30 – 1.30 P.M. pasta with any sauce	12.30 – 1.30 P.M. large baked potato plus 1 tablespoon filling
Meal 3	7 – 8 P.M. 4 oz fish in green sauce, 1 tablespoon of any vegetable or 1 potato	7 – 8 p.m. 4 oz chicken breast 1 tablespoon of any vegetable or 1 potato	7 – 8 p.m. 4 oz salmon, hollandaise sauce, 1 tablespoon potato or 1 apple

Drinks 7 – 10 drinks daily, including tea, coffee, and water. You may drink an contraceptive pill, HRT, or other hormonal treatment. Halve the number of whether diet or otherwise. Allow yourself one pint of milk a week.

NB 1 food is eating within the inner rim, 2 and 3 foods are eating within the not apply when eating orgasmically.

To lose weight rhythm 3	To lose weight rhythm 4	Eating orgasmically	Eating orgasmically
3 meals a day	3 meals a day	2 meals a day	2 meals in one long sitting
Thursday	**Friday**	**Saturday**	**Sunday**
7 A.M.	7.30 A.M.	9.30 A.M.	9.30 A.M.
11.30 P.M.	midnight	1 A.M.	11 P.M.
8.30 – 9 A.M.	8.30 – 9 A.M.		
5 – 5.30 P.M.	5 – 5.30 P.M.		
2 cups of tea/coffee	2 cups of tea/coffee	2 cups of tea/coffee	2 cups of tea/coffee
10 – 10.30 A.M. 1 banana	10 – 10.30 A.M. 1 banana		
1.30 – 2.00 P.M. medium sized baked potato, no filling	12.30 – 1.30 P.M. pasta with any sauce	12.30 – 1.30 P.M. 1 banana	2 – 4.30 P.M. traditional Sunday lunch of roast beef, dinner rolls, roast potatoes and vegetables followed by desserts
8.30 – 10.30 P.M. 3 course meal out	8 – 9 P.M. 4 oz chicken, mustard sauce, 1 tablespoon of any vegetable or 1 potato	8 – midnight dinner party	9 – 10 P.M. 1 fruit

additional 2 – 3 glasses of water if you need it unless you are on the alcoholic drinks you normally drink in a week. No or very few soft drinks –

normal rim. Counting foods and eating within the inner or normal rims do refer to this rhythm as the model rhythm because models use it to lose excess pounds in a hurry before photographic assignments. Be warned, though, that seven pounds lost rapidly in one week will not stay off unless you follow up with a few weeks on the gentle or control rhythms.

Like all rhythms, the quick rhythm needs to be tailored and fine-tuned to your individual requirements, but essentially it involves eating two normal rims or six foods a day, and eating orgasmically once or twice a week. In practice, if you work all week and socialize mainly at the weekend, then it is probably best to eat your six foods a day during the week, with nothing in between meals, and save your food orgasms for the weekend, always using the art of compensation, of course. If you are dining out in the week, then adapt the rhythm accordingly, but without increasing the overall amount of food you eat in the week. When you eat orgasmically or dine out, you will eat more, so it is important to eat within the inner rim at the meal before or after, or both.

The table on pages 114–15 shows the amount you should eat using the quick rhythm, and is an example of how you can adapt the quick rhythm to your lifestyle and your natural food rhythm.

If you have highly active taste buds, then you should restrict the variety of foods you eat in the early stages of losing weight. Eat filling foods and meals of a similar type, and avoid eating as soon as you get up.

You can lose seven pounds in your first week on the quick rhythm, especially if you have flattish rather than heaped tablespoons of vegetables and potatoes, and you cut right down on any alcoholic and soft drinks. Even though you will be eating small amounts of food, except when you knowingly eat orgasmically, you will still be eating a lot relative to the amount most dieters eat. To lose this amount in a week the old dieting way you would have to virtually starve! You cannot, however, sustain a weight loss of seven pounds in a week. This can only be achieved about once every six months.

The Gentle Rhythm

The gentle rhythm is similar to the quick rhythm, except that it allows you a more gentle start. It is suited to passive eaters and anyone who is not slimming to a particular deadline. This rhythm can be used indefinitely for losing weight, or you can alternate between the gentle and quick rhythms. Once you have got into the swing of it you can easily adapt and personalize this rhythm, although you may prefer to try some of the other slimming rhythms described in the next chapter.

You do not need to count foods on the gentle rhythm, but if you do, do not count so strictly. Allow yourself one or two foods a day more than you would on the quick rhythm, in other words seven or eight foods if you are counting, or one or two more servings within the inner rim (any amount which is less than three normal rims). Helpings of food may be a little more generous than on the quick rhythm, with larger portions of fish or meat, potatoes, and so on. But avoid eating in between meals, and if you do nibble or overeat, then miss a meal or go into the inner rim of your plate. As with the quick rhythm, allow yourself to eat orgasmically without restraint or guilt once or twice a week.

The table overleaf shows how to lose weight by the gentle method by counting foods, and a typical example of how the gentle rhythm can work in practice.

Example of the gentle rhythm

	Monday	**Tuesday**	**Wednesday**
Up	7 A.M.	7 A.M.	7 A.M.
Bed	10.30 P.M.	11 P.M.	10.30 P.M.
Start work	8.30 – 9 A.M.	8.30 – 9 A.M.	8.30 – 9 A.M.
Finish work	5 – 5.30 P.M.	5 – 5.30 P.M.	5 – 5.30 P.M.
8 A.M.	tea/coffee, 1 bowl cereal, a little milk	tea/coffee, 1 bowl cereal, a little milk	tea/coffee, 1 bowl cereal, a little milk
1 – 2 P.M.	baked potato plus filling	baked potato plus filling	pasta plus sauce
4 P.M.	banana	banana	apple
7 – 8 P.M.	fish in sauce, 1 tablespoon of potato or any vegetable	chicken kiev, 1 roast potato and 1 tablespoon vegetable	salmon en croûte, 1 tablespoon any vegetable

Drinks 7 – 10 drinks daily, including tea, coffee, and water. You may drink an contraceptive pill, HRT, or other hormonal treatment. Halve the amount of whether diet or otherwise. Allow yourself one pint of milk a week.

NB 1 food is eating within the inner rim, 2 and 3 foods are eating within the not apply when eating orgasmically.

Thursday	Friday	Saturday	Sunday
7 A.M.	7.30 A.M.	9.30 A.M.	9.30 A.M.
11.30 P.M.	midnight	1 A.M.	11 P.M.
8.30 – 9 A.M.	8.30 – 9 A.M.		
5 – 5.30 P.M.	5 – 5.30 P.M.		
tea/coffee, 1 bowl cereal, a little milk (circle, 1 dot)	tea/coffee, 1 apple (circle, 1 dot)	tea/coffee, bran/porridge, a little milk (circle, 1 dot)	tea/coffee, apple (circle, 1 dot)
taco or burrito (circle, 2 dots)	pasta plus sauce (circle, 2 dots)	cup of soup (circle, 1 dot)	traditional Sunday lunch (shaded circle)
apple (circle, 1 dot)	banana (circle, 1 dot)	banana (circle, 1 dot)	
3 course meal out (circle, 4 dots)	fish in sauce, 1 tablespoon vegetables plus 1 small potato (circle, 3 dots)	Dinner out or dinner party (shaded circle)	fruit (circle, 1 dot)

additional 2 – 3 glasses of water if you need it unless you are on the
alcoholic drinks you normally drink in a week. No or very few soft drinks –

normal rim. Counting foods and eating within the inner or normal rims do

Basic Rhythm – Week 1

Weigh Yourself

Weigh yourself, preferably first thing in the morning, either naked or wearing light clothing and no shoes. Find out your BMI (Body Mass Index) using the table on page 52. If it is over 25, calculate how many pounds/kilos you need to bring your BMI down to 25. If it is 25 or under, then aim to slim down and lose weight, perhaps using the gentle rhythm, which tends to be more suitable for slimmers at this stage, until you are within the range for your particular shape—ectomorph, mesomorph, or endomorph—or until you look and feel good. If your BMI is under 19 you are almost certainly under-weight, whatever your body shape, and should not lose any weight.

Which Rhythm?

The first thing to decide is which rhythm—quick or gentle—you want to start with. Obsessive personalities like me always want to lose weight as fast as possible, but remember Aesop's famous fable of the hare and the tortoise: slow and steady often wins the race! Be aware of when you need to slow down if you opt for the quick rhythm. If you start with the slow rhythm you can always shift gear upward into the quick rhythm once you have gained control and want to increase your slimming momentum.

Know Which Foods Satisfy You and Which Are Your Triggers!

Make a list of all the indulgent foods which trigger your taste buds into the mood to eat orgasmically. Until you have established your eating rhythm and are fully in control of what you eat, you cannot afford to eat orgasmically every day! Trigger foods are foods which, once you start, you cannot stop eating. Typical examples are chocolate, cookies, savory bits and pieces such as hors d'oeuvres, cheese puffs, salted roasted nuts of all kinds, chips, cheese and crackers, but we all have our own special triggers and it is as well to be aware of them. Add to your list when you find new triggers you were not aware of.

Make another list of filler foods—rice, pasta, noodles, potatoes, and so on—which fill or satisfy your hunger. Fullness and satisfaction stop you from overeating and give you the control which dieters so often lack.

Establish Your Basic Rhythm

Make a note of the times you normally get up, go to bed, work, eat, take the children to school and pick them up, make their tea, bath, and put the children to bed, socialize, any regular activities, and so on. Then plan your basic eating rhythm around the framework of your working day and your social life.

Decide how many meals a day you are going to eat (most of my clients eat the amount of two normal meals in three or four "sittings"), and what time you would like to eat them. If, for example, you start work at 9 A.M., and your work canteen opens mid-morning from 10.15–10.45 A.M., you could eat your first meal of the day then, especially if you have highly active taste buds. If you normally have tea with the children, or find it difficult to sit with them without eating yourself, then make that one of your mealtimes. Now start thinking about what you will eat. The following basic pattern of three meals a day works well for many people who work normal office hours or have young children—or both:

Meal One Sit and eat one or two foods—always make sure the food is filling, but not too indulgent, because you only have six or seven foods per day: for example, a toasted bagel or a muffin, and/or something light like a piece of fruit. Cut your fruit in slices—it tastes better and will seem more of a meal.

Remember that if you have highly passionate taste buds you should avoid eating as soon as you get up. If you stimulate your taste buds first thing in the day, you may end up eating *all* day! Do not indulge in too much variety because this will also stimulate your taste buds and tempt you to eat more and more until you overeat.

Meal Two Eat filling foods such as pasta with sauce, baked potato plus a filling (not melted cheese if you find it too fattening), any burger (without cheese which is very fattening), different-flavoured bar cookies. Reduce the variety of the food you eat for three to five consecutive days, especially if you have active taste buds. Eat pasta or a baked potato three days running, varying the sauce or filling if you like. Avoid foods and sauces that trigger you into eating more and more. I personally find chilli sauce with burgers or tacos highly orgasmic. Normally one burrito will satisfy me, but if I add chilli sauce then I can easily eat two or three followed by a bar of chocolate, even though I feel extremely full. Be aware of your triggers!

Meal Three As a general rule it is best to eat about six hours after your lunch. If you eat too early, you will be hungry when you go to bed, and if you eat too late, you will need to eat between lunch and dinner. For many people the third meal will be a family meal. If you and your family eat a starchy, filling lunch, this is ideally balanced by a hot dinner such as the traditional meat/fish and two veg combination, which provides a balance of proteins and carbohydrates. Choose from breasts of chicken, fish, meat, soya protein or beans, in any sauce, served with potatoes, rice, and/or vegetables.

Weekends Eat orgasmically if you work during the week and socialize mainly at the weekend. Never forget the art of compensation—you are paying back your fat loan!

Drinks Ideally keep to three and a half pints of fluid or about seven drinks daily, including tea, coffee, and water. Allow yourself a pint of milk—preferably skimmed or low-fat—a week (milk is a food), and halve the number of alcoholic and soft drinks you normally consume in a week. If you get thirsty, drink extra water.

Your basic eating rhythm needs to flow with the rhythm of your working life and your natural eating rhythm. The two forms of the basic rhythm given above are flexible enough to adapt to many lifestyles, but if you need more examples and suggestions then turn to the next chapter. Remember that you should go no longer than six hours if possible, or at the very most seven hours, without food.

Remember the Three Mental Exercises

1) Always say to yourself after eating: "I really enjoyed that."
2) Remember: "Hunger is losing weight."
3) Ask yourself: "Do I really want it?" If yes, then enjoy it. If you are not sure, then postpone it and eat it later if you still want it.

Fill in Your Food Diary

The times you get up, go to bed, start and finish work, and when and what you have to eat. Your food diary will begin to take shape as you start an eating and drinking rhythm geared to your lifestyle. By filling in the diary now you will find it easier to refine your basic rhythm as appropriate as you become daily more in touch with your natural eating rhythm.

Basic Rhythm – Week 2

Weigh Yourself

Weigh yourself at the same time of day either naked or wearing the same-weight clothes as you did at the beginning of Week 1.

If You Lost 5 – 7 lb in Week 1, You Need to Start Eating a Little More

Congratulations! You have made an excellent start but now you need to knowingly eat more. You will not be able to sustain such rapid weight loss and such small quantities of food without your body rebelling. If you try to, your body will rebel and you will find yourself bingeing. If you are happy with your Week 1 rhythm, then stay with it, but increase your helpings— allow yourself heaped instead of flattish serving spoons of vegetables, potatoes, and filler foods, and slightly larger portions of protein. If you are eating six foods a day and you are still very hungry, then add one more food.

If You Lost 2 – 4 lb on the Quick Rhythm or 1 – 3 lb with the Gentle Rhythm, Keep to the Same Amount of Food as Week 1

You too deserve congratulations on making an excellent start. If you are happy with your rhythm then carry on eating the same amount of food as in Week 1 to lose weight steadily, but change your menu.

If You Lost no Weight or You Gained Weight

If this is due to hormones—your period is due in a few days, or you are on HRT—then restrict your water, salt, and sugar intake, and keep to plain foods rather than indulgent ones which can trigger you into nonstop nibbling and eating.

If hormones are not to blame, then you need to review the amount you are eating, to pinpoint where the problem lies.

Have you been socializing and eating orgasmically when out without paying back? Have you been oversocializing and had no time to compensate? If you socialize and party frequently, then, until you feel in control, eat orgasmically only once or twice a week, avoid fattening foods and reduce the variety of foods you eat when partying. If you are at a buffet party or a party where plates of food or nibbles are being handed round with drinks, restrict yourself to two or three foods or nibbles only. If you are at a dinner party, avoid or go easy on preprandial nibbles and save yourself for the main meal. And remember, halve your alcohol consumption!

Have you been nibbling, bingeing or overeating without paying back? Eat simply—plain filler foods—and keep eating the same or similar foods. Too much variety will overstimulate your taste buds. Avoid moreish foods which trigger you into eating orgasmically unless you are out socializing and avoid them completely if you do not feel confident that you can stay in control. Do not eat first thing in the morning if it triggers you into eating all day. Postpone food for a couple of hours. If you are nibbling because you have too much food around you, then buy less, especially of foods you find indulgent. When you feel like nibbling, remember to ask yourself if you really want it. If your cravings for your trigger foods are uncontrollable, then go out and buy whatever it is you really desire. Eat to your heart's content—as much crispy fried bacon, crème brulée or as many Peppermint Patties as you want—but eat them as a meal and remember to compensate at the next mealtime. Say to yourself: "I have enjoyed it" after eating— especially after eating any food, or any amount of food, that you really feel deep down that you should not have eaten.

Example of the quiet rhythm

	Monday	Tuesday	Wednesday
9 – 10 A.M.	banana	banana	banana
12.30 – 1.30 P.M.	beef burrito or taco	beef burrito or taco	beef burrito or taco
7 P.M.	4 oz fish or chicken, 2 tablespoons vegetables	4 oz fish or chicken, 2 tablespoons vegetables	4 oz fish or chicken, 2 tablespoons vegetables
Drinks	7 drinks daily	7 drinks daily	7 drinks daily

Thursday	Friday	Saturday	Sunday
banana	banana		
beef burrito or taco	beef burrito or taco	banana	eat orgasmically
4 oz fish or chicken, 2 tablespoons vegetables	4 oz fish or chicken, 2 tablespoons vegetables	eat orgasmically	banana
7 drinks daily	7 drinks daily	7 drinks daily	7 drinks daily

127

Pay back by eating within the inner rim and telling yourself: "Hunger is losing weight." See also the nibbling rhythm (*page 136*) and the bingeing rhythm (*page 138*).

Are you overeating or drinking unknowingly? Many overweight people have what I call food amnesia, forgetting or underestimating the amount they eat and drink. Food amnesiacs often put their weight problems down to metabolism, but this is simply a myth (*see page 62*). Where food is scarce, and hunger a harsh reality, you do not see fat people. If you are overweight, and have not lost weight following the basic rhythm, then it is because, consciously or unconsciously, you have eaten more than your body needs, more than the maximum amount of two and a half normal rims a day. Remember, losing weight is all about quantity, quantity, quantity. Keep your food diary scrupulously, making a note whenever you eat and drink of whatever you eat and drink, and keep a check on the quantity you eat. And remember that when you are hungry you are losing weight.

Continue with the Three Mental Exercises

1) Always say to yourself after eating: "I really enjoyed that."
2) Remember: "Hunger is losing weight."
3) Ask yourself: "Do I really want it?" If yes, then enjoy it. If you are not sure, then postpone it and eat it later if you still want it.

Basic Rhythm – Week 3

Weigh Yourself

Weigh yourself at the same time of day either naked or wearing the same-weight clothes as you did at the beginning of Weeks 1 and 2.

If You Lost 2 – 3 lb in Week 2 with the Quick Rhythm or 1 – 2 lb with the Gentle Rhythm, Keep to the Same Amount of Food as Week 2

Well done! You can now see or sense your own eating and drinking rhythm emerging and you are beginning to look and feel good. If you feel in control, change your menu if you wish but keep to the same amounts. If you have very active taste buds, remember that too much variety is likely to stimulate you into eating more. Ring the changes at weekends or when you are out socializing, and know you will want to let your hair down and eat orgasmically! Keep on practicing the art of compensation.

If You Lost no Weight or Gained Weight

Analyze the reasons, checking through the possibilities listed under Week 2 and going through your food diary. Have you been hungry? Have you eaten beyond the rim and forgotten to return to the inner rim? If you are not sure why you have not lost weight, it may help to keep a more detailed food diary, making a note of when you practice the three mental exercises and of any feelings and emotions which affect the way and amount you eat, as well as the actual food you eat. For example, you could enter an **E** in your food diary every time you say: "I really enjoyed that" after eating, **Hu** for hunger, and **G** every time you feel guilty after eating. Likewise, **M** can stand for being in the mood to eat, **N** for nibbling, **Ho** for hormones—whether that means it is your time of the month or whether it stands for HRT, and so on.

Eat what you have in the freezer or the pantry, and buy only what you need, i.e., fruit, vegetables, and your filler foods.

Remember, There is No Need to Cheat!

You can eat whatever you fancy or need. The basic rhythm—like any other rhythm—is no more than a guide to eating. It is not a make-it-or-break-it set of rules. If you overdo it from time to time then pay back as soon as you can, either missing a meal or eating within the inner rim.

After Three Weeks

If you have been practicing the art of eating and compensating while you follow the basic rhythm, then at the end of three weeks you will have lost anything from seven to fourteen pounds if you have been using the quick rhythm, and between three and seven pounds using the gentle rhythm. You should now increase the amount you eat if you have been using the quick rhythm—but do not overdo it—say by switching to the slow rhythm for at least a couple of weeks. If you are on the gentle rhythm and you feel in control and would like to lose weight a little faster, then try the quick rhythm for two or three weeks.

As well as losing weight you will have been learning:

- to enjoy your food without feeling guilty;
- that allowing yourself to be hungry for a while before you eat gives you control. You may begin to welcome the return of hunger after being full, just as you enjoy the satisfaction of eating when you are hungry;
- that by postponing eating when you are in the mood to eat the urge often passes;
- that when you satisfy your body's needs by eating sufficient filler foods, and your taste buds by eating orgasmically, you are less likely to nibble between meals or to binge;
- to compensate or pay back when appropriate.

You have now started to eat orgasmically and before long will have completely mastered the art of eating. You will be liberated from the shackles of dieting and free to enjoy the magic of food as you shape up and lose weight. But beware the dangers that lurk for the unwary fattie paying back their fat loan...

When the initial enthusiasm which carries them through the first few weeks of their slimming regime begins to wane, many slimmers resort to nibbling in between meals and return to former eating patterns—old habits die hard. This is not to say they are weak-willed, it is just that the dieting mentality is reasserting itself—often with renewed vigor! This can be a hazardous time, but continuing to practice the three mental exercises will arm you against the dangers you confront in your final battle of the bulge, helping you to overcome your fat mind and the dieting mentality, and developing your new attitude toward food and drink.

The Danger that the Urge-To-Eat Will Lead to the Mood-To-Eat

Being in the mood to eat is a constant problem in the first stage of eating orgasmically, when you are trying to lose weight. We all, especially those of us who love eating and drinking, feel like nibbling from time to time. The trouble is that when you give in to this fancy for food, more often than not it does not end there. Chances are that once you pop one tasty little morsel into your mouth, you will get into the mood to eat. Your desire for food will increase and you will think you are hungry.

In fact the urge to eat can often be a false alarm or a passing whim, and does not necessarily mean that your body needs fuel. If this is so but you nevertheless start to nibble or pick at food, neither your taste buds nor your body will be satisfied. This is why people nibble a bit of this and a bit of that.

If you get the urge to eat something, remember the third mental exercise and ask yourself if you really want to eat. If the answer is "yes," then go ahead and eat enough of whatever it is that you want, need, or crave to feel satisfied. If you find yourself saying "yes" rather too often to your fancy for any one particular food, then eat it to the point of orgasm and, once satisfied, stop buying the food for a few weeks. If the answer is "maybe" or "no," postpone nibbling or eating.

If you find yourself continually nibbling and picking at this and that, it may be that you are not eating enough filler food or that you have not eaten orgasmically. If you wish to stop nibbling, use the nibbling rhythm (*page 136*), then return to Week 1.

The Dangers of Hunger Pangs—and the Lack of Them: Getting the Balance Right

Many of the long-term overweight, especially those whose parents were rationed during the war years, have been conditioned to keep their stomachs full and to polish off everything on their plates, whether they really want it or not. As a result they never feel hungry, their blood sugar levels are always high and they become—and stay—fat. Dieting programs and gurus often reinforce this "fear" of hunger, promising dieters that by following their particular regime, they will lose weight without experiencing hunger. This is a fix.

The real truth is that it is natural and normal to feel hungry, but not starving, in between meals. It is also conducive to good health and a balanced diet. Hunger plays an important part in communicating not only that the body is in need of food, and that it will dip into your reserves of fat if it does not receive nourishment, but also what kind of food the body requires. It is a strange but true fact that fat people can suffer from malnutrition. This is because, by not allowing themselves to feel hungry, they miss their bodies' signals for particular foods. The result can be an unbalanced diet that does not provide important nutrients.

The way to tune into your body's needs and to shed excess fat is to condition your mind to flow with the natural rhythm of the body, which is to be hungry...full...hungry...full. Remember, hunger is losing weight. After a few days, when you have got into a rhythm, your hunger pangs will subside and you will begin to enjoy the feeling of mild hunger as you become sensitive to the signals of your body. You will also enjoy your food more!

The more you are hungry, and the less you are full, the more weight you will lose, but beware of becoming too hungry. Make sure you go no longer than six, or an absolute maximum of seven, waking hours without food. Getting too hungry usually ends up in a binge as the body screams out its need for fuel.

The Danger of Food Obsession

To be in control of what you eat and drink, you need to have a balanced attitude toward food. If you are an active fattie, you will always be thinking of food, especially if you have been a dieter. Many passive dieters also become obsessed with food.

The best way to put an end to food obsession is to allow yourself to relax and enjoy everything you choose to eat and drink, eating orgasmically when you are triggered off by food you find moreish. Never feel guilty about eating—and especially not about "unscheduled" eating; never feel as if you are "breaking the rules" or in any way "failing." Eating orgasmically is not a diet. It is a way of life which involves paying back your fat loan if you have overborrowed by practicing the art of compensation.

Every time you eat, remember to tell yourself that you have enjoyed it, especially when you eat foods you once regarded as "forbidden." You will be amazed how effective and powerful the simple expedient of mental suggestions can be.

Week 4 Onward

Your own eating and drinking pattern will have emerged by the time you have been practicing the art of eating and compensating for three weeks, and you will find that you cannot eat as much as you did previously because your eating capacity will already have been reduced.

From now on, begin consciously to tune into your own body rhythm. The more sensitive to its signals you become, the more you will find you can eat and drink:

> whatever you want
> whenever you want
> wherever you want
> however much you want
> and most important
> stop when you have had enough.

You will become increasingly aware of what and how much your body needs to eat and when. You will enjoy your food without restraint and be able to indulge your desire for the foods you love in whatever situation you wish—over a business dinner at a posh restaurant, alone at home, or out with friends—until you reach food satisfaction or, beyond, to food orgasm.

Weigh Yourself

Continue to weigh yourself once a week. When you get within seven pounds of your ideal weight, the weight at which you look and feel your best, weight loss generally slows down.

Relax and take it easy, and consider changing to the control rhythm (*page 162*).

Which Rhythm?

If you have been using the quick rhythm for three weeks and you have lost 10 pounds or more, increase the amount you are eating. Whatever rhythm you are using, ask yourself if you are happy and relaxed with it. If not, modify it as appropriate or turn to the next chapter for alternative slimming rhythms and go straight into the rhythm of your choice. You should not be too hungry, feel deprived or dissatisfied. It is only when you are at ease with your pattern of eating and drinking that you can modify your eating habits. Your aim is to permanently alter your eating behavior from that of the fattie, who cannot stop eating once she or he starts, to that of the naturally slim, able to eat anything and everything they want without gaining weight because they stop eating when they have had enough and pay back when they overdo it. Unlike slim dieters and food phobics, who often just pick and poke at their food, so worried about the fattening effects of food that they can never enjoy good food, natural slimmies enjoy their food, employing the art of eating and drinking, as well as the art of compensation to keep them in shape.

Remember the Three Mental Exercises

Continue to practice the three mental exercises—practice really does make perfect! During the early weeks you are almost bound to revert to your old eating habits at times—the dieting mind is unyielding. You will start to count calories or feel guilty about forbidden food, and you will nibble or binge. If other strategies fail, then try the nibbling or bingeing rhythms overleaf.

135

The Nibbling Rhythm

Everyone experiences days when they feel like nibbling, and there is nothing wrong with having a nibbling day. Listen to your body and your taste buds, and ask yourself if you really want to nibble. If the answer is yes, then go ahead. Nibble away and enjoy it. If you want to carry on, then do so instead of a meal or meals—you may not lose weight but you will not gain too much. Nibble all day if you feel like it, and if you end up bingeing, relax, enter into it, and enjoy that too. Just remember to tell yourself as you nibble, pick, or binge that you are enjoying it. Return to within the inner rim and pay back as necessary later on.

When You Want to Stop Nibbling

Nibbling is usually a sign that you have failed to satisfy your body's nutritional requirements or that your taste buds are frustrated, because you have not eaten orgasmically. It follows that the simplest way to stop nibbling is to satisfy mind and body with as much of whatever it is that you desire or need. Filling food is more satisfying to the body than anything else— a large potato (baked, roast, boiled, sauté, or chipped) with whatever filling or sauce that you fancy, or a small loaf of bread with whatever spread you want, and you will surely stop. Even though your stimulated taste buds may linger and niggle a little, I can assure you that your stomach simply will not be able to accommodate anything more after all your nibbling and filler food on top!

Example of the nibbling rhythm

	Saturday	Sunday	Monday
Up	7 A.M.	7 A.M.	7 A.M.
Bed	11 P.M.	11 P.M.	11 P.M.
Start work	9 A.M.	9 A.M.	
Finish work	5 P.M.	5 P.M.	
Morning	nibbling: cookies, chocolate, dried fruit	nibbling: chips, peanuts, chocolate	pay back
Afternoon	out for meal: small main course, indulgent dessert	baked potato	nibbling: dates, chocolate cake, chocolate kisses
Drinks	7 drinks daily	7 drinks daily	7 drinks daily

137

The Bingeing Rhythm

The potency of the dieting mentality should never be dismissed or underestimated and, as a former dieter and binger, you cannot expect an overnight transformation. You will continue to binge now and again until you transform your binges into food orgasms, and your dieting mentality into an orgasmic one. Remember, bingeing is an inhibited food orgasm: as the slave rather than the master of the food you eat, out of control as well as out of shape, you hardly dared eat the "forbidden" foods you loved and craved, let alone eat enough of them to peak. The result was often that you ended up eating anything and everything, but not what you really wanted—and, if you did eat what you really wished for, guilt spoiled your enjoyment.

If you know you are going to binge, give in to it and *enjoy* it. If you can, stop for a moment before you get going and ask yourself: "What do I really want?" Then go for it—your favorite chocolate, a pound of cheese, a giant packet of peanuts—and eat all you want. After eating, tell yourself that you enjoyed it, and pay back with two inner rims—for example two baked potatoes—the next day. (*See page 174.*)

When You Cannot Stop Eating or Bingeing, Use the Bingeing Rhythm

Buy an exaggerated amount of whichever food you most crave, for example 5 lb of cheese (one kind), bacon or chocolate (one sort only), or five loaves of bread. Eat nothing else (you can have cookies or bread with your cheese if you wish). Each time you feel the urge to eat, bring out your huge cheese, or make stacks of bacon sandwiches, and eat until you are completely satisfied. Remember to tell yourself that you have enjoyed it after each session.

Once you have polished off or made serious inroads into your stash of chocolate, cheese, or bacon, go out and buy enough to replace whatever you have eaten, so you have the same quantity you started out with.

Repeat the process so long as you cannot stop eating or bingeing. If possible, ask yourself each time before you eat if you really want it. If the answer is yes, bring out the whole cheese or a substantial quantity of whatever goodie you have elected to binge on and eat it to your heart's content. If no, or maybe, then postpone eating for the moment. By postponing or putting a temporary halt to your binge, even for a few seconds, you are learning how to apply the brakes. In other words you are learning control. With practice those few seconds in which you stopped eating and your taste buds stopped being titillated will turn into a few minutes, then a few hours. You will have learned to stop eating. As time goes by this will become easier and easier. Practice makes perfect.

After a day or two—most of my patients stay on the bingeing rhythm for a day—your taste buds will be utterly satiated with cheese or chocolate fudge cake or whatever your chosen food is, and you will have lost your obsession with it. You will be able to eat as much of it as you like without guilt and so have a healthier attitude to it. Once you have reached the point of satiety, return to the art of compensation and remind yourself that "hunger is losing weight." (*See page 174.*)

To Regain Control after Bingeing and Start Losing Weight

Follow the quiet rhythm for a week, eating the same or similar-tasting food every day, with as little variety as possible, but eating orgasmically once or twice in the week. This will calm your taste buds and give your overstretched stomach muscles a rest. Then return to your basic rhythm if you are slimming or your control rhythm if you are near or have reached your perfect shape. If and when you binge again, your reduced eating capacity will mean that you consume less on a binge than you would have done before. Your binges will turn into food orgasms and you will enjoy them! (*See pages 126, 174.*)

If You Stop Losing Weight

If you stop losing weight before you have reached your ideal weight—the weight at which you look and feel good, and your BMI is still above the range for your body type, then it is almost certainly because you have unconsciously increased the amount you are eating and drinking. Many of my patients come to me after six or eight weeks complaining that they have stopped losing weight. Invariably it turns out that, without really being aware of it, they are eating more. If you keep increasing the size of your heaped tablespoon of vegetables and potatoes, for example, "a little more" will soon add up to "a lot more." Remember that you are paying off a loan, and every penny counts. If you are not losing weight it is because you are not paying back sufficiently. Even though you may have reduced your eating capacity on the basic rhythm, you can soon reverse this if you start to overeat without compensating.

Return to your basic rhythm, eating six to eight foods, and keeping to the same or similar foods, for example eating a banana every day for breakfast, pasta or a baked potato every day for lunch, four ounces of fish or chicken for dinner, and so on. This will help calm down your taste buds, especially if you have a passion for food and love eating. Hunger is losing weight.

If you go back to the quick rhythm, as most people who have been obsessive dieters will, with flattish tablespoons of vegetables, then you will probably lose in the region of three to five pounds in the first week if you have been nibbling or bingeing in the meantime. You will not be able to maintain this rate of weight loss. Your body will need more fuel after the first week and to keep in control you will need consciously to eat a little more.

Relax and take it easy if you prefer to eat more and lose weight more slowly. Just think: if you lose one pound a week continuously, that amounts to 52 pounds in a year—well over three and a half stones! It takes time to get into shape, especially if you have been out of shape for a long time. Relax and learn how your body works and what it needs. There is no race to regain your ideal shape, and even if there were, you can only win by going at the right pace for you. Remember the story of the hare and the tortoise?

When You Feel Out of Balance, Out of Sorts, or Out of Control

Once you have begun to tune in to your own body rhythm, your mind and body will begin to flow in the same direction and, more often than not, will be in perfect harmony. You will look and feel good, and you will be in control. But life changes, good fortune, bad fortune, emotional ups and downs, or even plain boredom are sure to strike every now and again and disturb your equilibrium. At times like this you are more likely to eat erratically, and to nibble, snack, graze, binge, or eat orgasmically—rather too often!

If, as a result, you are not in the mood to lose weight, or you feel that you or your body needs a rest, then let go, relax, and eat and drink what you like. You can still, without any effort, maintain your current weight or let it fluctuate by no more than a few pounds by what I call terracing.

The Terracing Rhythm

Terracing is for slimmers who need a rest from slimming for one reason or another—and after you have been slimming for a while your body may have had enough for the time being, even if your mind is not in agreement! Although eating orgasmically is a natural and easy way to slim and stay slim, it is not easy to keep on paying back a loan nonstop. Sometimes you need a short break or a good vacation.

When you use the terracing rhythm you are basically maintaining your current weight, but allowing it to fluctuate by a few pounds. You do this by eating orgasmically to satisfy your body and your taste buds, and compensating when possible. Soon mind and body will be back in sync, and you will be back on course for losing weight.

Do not worry if you put on a few pounds in the meantime—they will soon be lost when you return to the inner rim and start paying back.

Keep practicing the three mental exercises, and stop buying, fattening foods and start to pay back as soon as you feel you can.

Different Rhythms for Different Rimes

Eating orgasmically is not just about losing weight and staying slim. It is about tuning into your own rhythms, and the rhythms of life: when to lose weight, when to stay in shape, when to gain weight.

The annual cycle of seasons, festivals, and holidays call for differing rhythms as do the seasons of your life.

Turn to the next chapter for alternative examples of slimming rhythms that you can adapt and shape to your own lifestyle, and to Chapter 9 for rhythms which will keep you slim and take you through the Christmas season, Easter, and holidays.

Good luck—and enjoy it!

8

More Slimming Rhythms

The basic rhythm, with a bit of fine-tuning, works wonderfully for anyone who works normal office hours, and for those involved in bringing up children and the care of the house. For some, though, in particular people who work irregular hours, it is unsuitable.

This chapter gives examples of rhythms designed for a variety of working patterns, lifestyles, tastes, and age ranges. Whether you are looking for a rhythm to start you off eating orgasmically, or whether you have been using the basic rhythm for a few weeks and want to establish a rhythm more suited to you, the examples in this chapter may help. Remember, though, that the eventual aim is not to copy someone else's rhythm, but to establish a rhythm unique to you, in tune with your individual body rhythm and lifestyle. While you are at the stage of losing weight rather than maintaining your weight and staying in shape, this may involve some trial and error, but I can assure you that once you have acquired the art of eating—which you can do by getting into any suitable rhythm—it will happen!

Whichever rhythm you adopt to begin with, after a few weeks you will not only have lost weight, but you will be more sensitive to your body's food signals, eating when you are hungry, stopping when you have had enough, and compensating when you overdo it. At the same time you will be learning the art of balancing the nutritional needs of your body with your natural desire to eat orgasmically at times and to indulge your fancy for the foods you love. Your rhythm will evolve along with your new attitude to food and your new eating habits and before long, almost without your knowing it, you will have developed your own individual food rhythm—a rhythm which will vary and change along with variations in your routine, changes in lifestyle, and other circumstances.

The sample rhythms in this chapter come under five main headings:

Irregular working hours
Night worker's rhythm
Shift worker's rhythm
Publican's rhythm
High flier's rhythm

Ages and stages of life
Children's rhythm
Teenager's rhythm
Student's rhythm

Special diets and special foods
Vegetarian and vegan rhythms
Chocolate lover's rhythm

Special and unusual lifestyles
Exercise rhythm
Partygoer's rhythm

Once you have decided which rhythm is most appropriate for you, go back to Chapter 7. The same principles apply to all rhythms, with the exception that growing children and teenagers can lose weight on three normal meals, or nine foods a day (which should be divided up into four or five smaller meals), whereas adults need less—two to two-and-a-half normal rims, or six to eight foods a day, depending on whether you want to lose weight quickly or gently.

Weigh yourself once a week, practice the three mental exercises, fill in your food diary, and get to know your triggers! Allow yourself seven to ten drinks daily, with extra water if necessary unless you are on hormonal treatment such as the birth control pill or HRT. If you have any problems—for example you lose no weight or you gain weight—then follow the advice given in Chapter 7 listed under Weeks 2 and 3.

Irregular Working Hours

Some jobs, for example those of health care professionals, shift workers, people working in the entertainment industry, restaurant and bar staff, involve irregular, unsocial, or unpredictable working hours. You may have to get up very early, and work very long hours, and your working pattern may be constantly changing, each day different to the one before. For you it is particularly important to eat the right amount at the right time if you are to avoid nibbling and picking throughout the day.

Because your hours are irregular, you, above all, need to establish your own individual rhythm and be able to change or adapt it as necessary to fit changeable working hours. The rhythms below are examples only, intended not to be followed just as they stand but as a guide to help you work out and establish a rhythm that suits your unique requirements.

Night Worker's Rhythm

Whether you work in a busy night club or as a solitary night watchman, whether you are a doctor on call or nursing an invalid who needs round-the-clock care, your days and nights are topsy-turvy, and your working hours often long and lonely. Eating keeps you going and helps pass time when every minute seems like an hour. Losing weight may seem an almost impossible feat.

Learning to eat orgasmically and practicing the art of compensation will make it easier than you dreamed it could be. Once you learn to listen to what your body needs and find the best time to eat both in your working and social life, then you will certainly lose weight.

Be sure to eat a warm, filling meal before you begin work, followed by another filling meal during the night, keeping the intervals between meals to a maximum of six hours. Food satisfaction is essential not only to keep you going physically, but to sustain you psychologically through the long night. A cup of hot soup when you finish work, and before you go to bed, can be very comforting.

Shift Worker's Rhythm

The pattern of shift workers' hours often changes on a regular basis, so one week you may be on a morning shift, rising at the crack of dawn or before to get to work in the early hours, the next on afternoon shift, followed by a week on nights. You may even work more than one shift a day.

Because of your erratic hours, you need to have a highly flexible rhythm, or a separate rhythm for each shift. You may also need more than the amount of two normal rims, or six foods a day. I recommend that you start eating orgasmically by establishing a rhythm or rhythms allowing you to eat the amount of two-and-a half normal rims, or seven to eight foods a day, which you may spread out into three to five meals. Once you get into a suitable rhythm, you will lose weight steadily and easily.

MORNING SHIFT

If you are working on the morning shift, eat a filler food for breakfast before work if you wish, except if you are an active eater, in which case avoid eating first thing in the morning as it will only make you want to carry on all day. Eat a filling meal —bring it to work with you if there is no cafeteria—when you have been up for five or six hours, and enjoy your main meal in the late afternoon or early evening, a few hours before you go to bed.

AFTERNOON/NIGHT SHIFTS

Be sure to eat a filling meal before you begin work on the afternoon and night shifts—filler food is your salvation during unsociable working hours, and will help you to avoid nibbling when you are on the job. Eat another filling meal halfway through your shift, and a light meal before you go to bed.
See also the night worker's rhythm, opposite.

Barperson's Rhythm

You have a busy and demanding job, often working all hours with just a few hours' break in between opening times. Your hospitality and sociability are second to none as you welcome and serve your customers, while keeping an eye on the smooth running of the establishment. Food and drink surround you. Even if you resist the temptation to help yourself, your customers frequently offer you a drink.

However, recent research shows that alcohol dulls the HSM or hunger-satiety mechanism (*see page 69*), the feedback system which signals when we need to eat and when we have had enough by generating sensations of hunger or fullness. This means that you are likely to eat more if you drink before rather than during or after a meal, so it matters not only how much you drink, but when you drink.

Halve your alcohol intake, and be sure to keep within the recommended weekly allowance. As you probably know, a glass of red wine a day has been shown to reduce the risk of coronary heart disease, but it is all too easy to lose track of how much you drink if your glass is constantly being topped up. You may find it easier to monitor your drinks if you start a new glass each time, and if you find it difficult to drink just one or two glasses a day, then consider setting aside one or two days a week as alcohol-free days. Try to drink slowly, avoiding neat spirits. Diluting them with water, ice, or tonic makes them last much longer.

To avoid nibbling bar snacks and other foods while you work, and to be sure your HSM is in full working order at and around mealtimes, make sure that you have a filling meal before opening. After closing in the evening have a light meal such as a cup of soup or a piece of fruit before bed.

Once you have got into a steady eating and drinking rhythm, you will be able to relax and enjoy eating orgasmically on your nights and days off, compensating when you can.

High Flier's Rhythm

Your ambitious approach to life and work mean that you are constantly on the go, and the boundaries between working and socializing are blurred. Whether you are in business, banking, or finance, an aspiring politician or a partner in a law firm, entertaining is important to you as a way to network and build up connections and contacts. Breakfast meetings at five-star hotels, and business lunches and dinners at top-rated restaurants with outstanding cellars, afford you ample opportunity to eat orgasmically – perhaps more often than is good for you! Even when you are not out to impress, but socializing purely with partners or old friends, you still like to live—and eat—well.

Compensation is the name of the game for you. Aim to eat orgasmically twice a week, more often if the occasion calls for it, though you may need to rethink this if too many orgasmic meals are overstimulating your taste buds. After eating orgasmically, pay back with an inner rim, or one food only, at the next one or two meals if your busy schedule of socializing and business entertaining allows for it. Even if you are an active eater, enjoy the pleasures of bacon and eggs at your breakfast meeting, and compensate later. Halve your alcohol intake and if you have several business lunches or dinners a week, avoid drinking more than once a day, and have one or two courses only, except when you decide to eat orgasmically. Finally, remember that, for you, acquiring the art of compensation is what losing weight hinges on.

One businessman following the rhythm on page 180 lost four pounds in one week.

Ages and Stages of Life

Nutritional requirements vary throughout life, but establishing an eating rhythm and a balanced diet are important at *all* stages of life. Regular mealtimes will help young children to tune into their own rhythms from an early age, and help them avoid the misery of growing up overweight.

Teenagers are beginning to experiment with food, as with everything else, and should be encouraged and allowed to indulge their passions and whims—whether for a vegetarian diet, very popular with teenagers, or for experimental cooking—so long as they keep in rhythm and have a nutritionally sound diet overall. *No* teenager wants or needs to enter their adult life overweight—so enter the diet-free zone now! Teenagers who have learned the art of eating orgasmically will have a head start when they become students, as they will be completely tuned into their own eating rhythms. Student days can be wild and erratic, and for you the art of compensation is especially important. Eating filler foods will save you money, too.

By the time we enter our 60s and beyond, we are more likely to thrive on an orderly routine—foodwise as well as in the rest of our lives. A balanced diet and enough sleep helps keep you fit and full of energy well into old age—and if you need to lose weight, the basic rhythm is perfect for you.

Children's Rhythm (3–12)

Fat children are often the butt of jokes at school and left out of all the fun and games. Preschool children may not be concerned about their weight, but you should aim to slim them down before they start school, if they are overweight. School-age children will be all too aware of their size compared with others and frequently find being overweight a source of embarrassment and distress.

The best way to help your child is to get them into rhythm. Lack of any rhythm or routine inevitably results in a higher consumption of chips, cookies, candy and ice creams. There is nothing wrong with allowing children to eat chocolate and other fun foods—children need to eat orgasmically too—so long as they do not form their staple diet. Remember, it is the quantity of food you eat, not the kind, that makes you fat. If your children eat unscheduled "snacks," they are actually eating a meal, so count it as one and do not expect them to eat lunch or dinner soon after. Children who eat nutritious food in between meals, then regular meals on top, inevitably get fat.

That said, growing children should never be encouraged to lose weight fast, any more than they should be encouraged to diet. The aim with children is not so much to help them lose weight, as to slow down their weight gain so that as they grow in height, they slim down.

Keep to a rhythm of four or five small meals a day, and a maximum of three normal rims (less for very small children) or nine foods a day, making sure that the child eats a balanced mix of nutrients—carbohydrates, proteins (very important for growth), fats, vitamins, and minerals. Tune into your child's rhythms, and never force children to eat food they do not want or when they are not hungry. If your child cannot finish his or her lunch or tea, do not make them. If he or she does not want breakfast, accept it. A banana or a cookie at breaktime, or even a packet of chips or a bar of chocolate, will keep him or her going until lunch. To avoid nibbling and picking after school, make sure children have a filler food such as a bowl of pasta or a baked potato with baked beans soon after they get home from school. This may be followed by a light meal before bedtime.

Last but not least, remember that children, just like adults, need to eat orgasmically—but not at every mealtime! If your child has favorite foods, include them two or three times a week as a part or the whole of his or her meal.

Teenager's Rhythm *(12–18)*

No—I do not believe in baby fat. Youth bestows a fullness and roundness which age robs us of, but to be fat is another matter. This is a time when you are experimenting with looks, style, and developing your personal identity. Feeling good and being in shape is important and gives you the confidence you need.

There are three main genetically inherited body types (*see Chapter 3*), and as you get into your early teens your natural shape will emerge. Never try to alter your natural shape—the endomorph who aspires to being an ectomorph will never succeed, but may well develop eating disorders by trying. Accept, enjoy, and make the most of your individual body type by becoming *your* correct or ideal shape.

If you are overweight, use the basic rhythm and adapt it to your lifestyle. Establish an eating rhythm of three or four meals a day, to the amount of two-and-a-half normal platefuls, or seven to eight foods, daily. Avoid breakfast first thing in the morning if it sets you off eating all day, and ask your parents to help you by not filling the house with tempting foods you do not need. Be sure to eat a filling meal when you get back from school—this will stop the fatal nibbling and picking which makes you put on weight. Learn the art of compensation and remember the inner rim!

Student's Rhythm

Becoming a student may mean leaving home and making your first real bid for freedom. You are now officially an adult, and this is a time for self-expression as you enjoy this new-found freedom.

Routine can easily go out the window in the absence of the regular meals you got at home and at school, and as new priorities fill your life. Making new friends and being sociable may involve spending more time and money in the snack bar than in the cafeteria and you may find yourself nibbling, snacking, grazing, or gorging all day and partying all night.

To lose weight it is vital that you discover an eating and drinking rhythm which you can keep to. Avoid breakfast if it triggers you into nibbling all day or a binge, and stoke up on filler foods—they are cheap as well as satisfying. A large baked potato with a heaped serving spoon of baked beans, tuna, or cheese will see you through five or six hours. A square meal of fish or meat and two vegetables is well balanced and will give you the energy your still-growing body needs. Two or three bars of chocolate instead of a meal now and again will not only satisfy your taste buds but keep your sugar levels high.

Halve your alcohol intake, and cut down on soft drinks, even of the low-calorie variety. Perfect the art of compensation and you will enjoy your student life as you lose weight yet still eat and drink without guilt.

Special Diets and Special Foods

Throughout the world people adopt special diets or avoid certain foods on religious, humanitarian, or health grounds. Others, like myself, develop food fads, fancies, and cravings that just *have* to be fulfilled. We will nibble, binge, and be discontent until they are. Chocolate lovers like myself sometimes need to indulge to the point of complete satiety to avoid nibbling. Food fads and cravings are usually short-lived, so long as they are satisfied, but I still remember the story of the British schoolboy who made the headlines in 1997 after breaking his four-year diet of eating nothing but jelly sandwiches! Amazingly, it appeared that he had not suffered nutritionally—and he certainly did not have a weight problem.

I would not recommend such a diet to anyone—and few people are so extreme or restricted in their tastes. Most special diets and food cravings can easily be incorporated into the basic rhythm, but be sure always to balance your diet nutritionally.

Vegetarian and Vegan Rhythms

There are many excellent reasons for becoming a vegetarian, although losing weight is not one of them. Most vegetarians include dairy produce and eggs in their diets, but vegans exclude all animal produce, while fruitarians eat nothing but fruit. The latter are beyond the scope of this book.

A vegetarian or vegan diet can be a very healthy one, but you need to be careful to ensure an adequate protein, vitamin and mineral intake. This is especially true in the case of teenagers who sometimes lack—or their parents may lack—awareness of the nutritional issue involved.

Eggs and dairy produce are good sources of protein for most vegetarians, but vegans need to combine beans with cereals and grains, as non-animal sources of protein do not contain all the essential amino acids the human body requires. Vegetarians and vegans also need to be sure that they are getting the other nutrients they need—vitamin and mineral deficiencies, particularly iron and vitamin B_{12}, are often found in vegetarians.

Fortunately there are many books available which explain how you can eat healthily as a vegetarian or vegan, and so long as you take steps to ensure a balanced diet, you can follow either form of the basic rhythm described in Chapter 7, adapting it to your convenience.

Chocolate Lover's Rhythm

Is it the taste, the texture, the smell, the look, or merely the thought of chocolate that triggers chocolate lovers such as myself into such a frenzy of desire? Once I have even the tiniest nibble I need more and more until I am completely orgasmic and my chocolate taste buds are replete.

The amount I need varies, but I need more than one bar of chocolate with nuts to peak. I need at least two normal bars or one family-sized bar before I am truly satisfied and able to stop. But for some all it takes is just one or two exquisite Belgian chocolates after dinner.

Chocolate lovers like myself, who need chocolate in quantity, may like to try my chocolate rhythm on page 184, for one or two weeks.

Special and Unusual Lifestyles

Unfortunately there is not enough space in this book to cover all the many wonderful and unusual lifestyles that I have come across during all my years of practice and treating overweight patients. However, in my line of business I do come across a lot of exercise fans and fanatics, so I have developed a rhythm, below, especially for them.

For the rest, suffice it to say that with a bit of ingenuity everyone can establish a rhythm, even if it is a rhythm marked by change and flexibility. If yours is an erratic lifestyle because you travel a lot, because you are involved in creative projects that come and go, or for any other reason, then perfecting the art of compensation is key to getting and keeping in shape. The same is true of all great socializers, socialites, and partygoers.

Exercise Rhythm

Regular exercise—20 to 30 minutes three or four times a week—is very beneficial to your health and looks, keeping you fit as well as youthful-looking by increasing the blood flow to the skin and the rest of your body. Exercise is instrumental in lifting depression, it can help lower your stress levels and plays a part in relieving and preventing many health problems. It can also help you lose weight, though not if you increase the amount you eat.

To lose weight through exercise you also need to practice the art of eating, and whatever exercise you do—walking, jogging, running, swimming, dancing, aerobics, weight training, step—do not become obsessive about it. Obsessive exercising is just as harmful as obsessive dieting, and if an injury or other circumstances force you to stop for a while, the weight piles on again, just as it does in the case of dieters who stop dieting.

If you are an exercise fanatic—in other words, you exercise five or more times a week, for about an hour or so each time—use the basic rhythm but make sure you eat one filler food, say, a banana or a roll, an hour or so before strenuous exercise (unless you are exercising first thing in the morning), and eat a filling food such as a baked potato or pasta afterward.

Even if you enjoy more moderate exercise two or three times a week, it is still a good idea to eat some starchy food an hour beforehand, followed by your usual meal afterward.

Partygoer's Rhythm

If your life is a frenzied social whirl of cocktail parties, dinner parties, business dinners, and charity functions, then you will need to keep an especially watchful eye on your figure. You want to look your best at all occasions while enjoying the delicious foods and wines that your lifestyle offers you.

Your salvation lies in the art of compensation. Pay back with one or two inner rims each time you eat orgasmically, and eat only two or three different kinds at buffets and parties, avoiding any you find very moreish unless you have decided to eat orgasmically.

Avoid breakfast if it triggers you into eating all day, and particularly if your taste buds are already highly stimulated from the previous day. Halve your alcoholic intake, making sure to keep within the recommended guidelines. Try not to drink alcohol more than once a day, and avoid drinking on an empty stomach. If you must keep a drink in your hand at all times, alternate between wine and mineral water.

Nobody is born or destined to be fat. Whatever your lifestyle, whatever your age, and whatever your work, you can and will lose weight when you change your attitude to eating and drinking, and learn to enjoy it.

Through acquiring the art of eating you will not only lose weight, but, unlike 95 per cent of dieters, you will keep it off. Turn to the next chapter for the control rhythm and other rhythms which will keep you in shape for the rest of your life.

9

How to Stay in
Shape Forever

Figures show that between 95 percent and 98 percent of people who lose weight by dieting put it all back on again, and more, often ending up heavier than before they ever began. Why? Either because once they stop dieting they go back to the eating patterns which made them overweight in the first place or, worse, because they get caught in the dieting trap, developing the dieting mentality and the yoyo weight syndrome, as we have seen in Chapter 2. Diets simply do not address the key question of what happens once you reach your ideal shape. The only option if you want to stay slim is to carry on dieting—reinforcing further your fat mind which causes your weight to swing.

Fatness and obesity are symptoms of overeating, not the disorder itself, and dieters fail to stay slim because dieting is the wrong prescription. Dieting may rid you of your fat—usually temporarily—but it leaves the underlying causes of the problem untreated and creates another problem: the fat mind and all the guilt and obsession that go with it. Eating orgasmically, in contrast, is a way of life—not a diet, more a dieter's dream come true! It is a holistic approach to losing weight and, above all, to staying in shape—permanently.

Eat with Relish, Compensate with Style...

Once you have lost weight and got into shape by eating orgasmically for a few weeks or months, you will have begun to acquire the art of eating—combining the food flair and appreciation of the gutsy food lover with the ability of the slimmie to compensate with style. You will feel full more quickly than you used to because your eating capacity is reduced, and you will be able to stop eating when you wish—even leaving food on your plate when you have had enough—something you could never do before. You will be the master of what you eat and drink, not the slave, increasing in confidence as your fat mind loses its grip and you enjoy peak food experiences without guilt.

...But Beware the Potency of the Fat Mind

The usual reason dieters fail to stay slim is because of their fat minds which diets have failed to treat. The weight problems of Elizabeth Taylor are legendary. This celebrated film star personifies the perils of dieting and the damage caused by the dieting mentality, alternately dieting and then ballooning out of shape, often in a matter of weeks. Instead of eating orgasmically, giving free rein to her passionate and colorful taste buds, and then compensating to stay in shape, she condemned herself to dieting and guiltily bingeing as a way of life. She has rarely been in shape for long at a time.

Even if you have been eating orgasmically for several weeks or months, beware, if you are a former dieter, not to be caught off guard by the sudden reappearance of fat old ways of thinking. The potency of the fat mind should never be underestimated. It can return as if from the dead when your defences are down, especially as you approach and reach your ideal shape. And although your mind and body will be in equilibrium and well synchronized most of the time, there will always be times when you go out of control and out of sync. Whenever this happens, remember and practice the three mental exercises:

1) Always say to yourself after eating: "I really enjoyed that."
2) Remember: "Hunger is losing weight."
3) Ask yourself: "Do I really want it?" If yes, then enjoy it. If you are not sure, then postpone and eat it later if you still want it.

Quantity…Quantity…Quantity…

Keeping in shape is all about the amount of food you eat. If you eat normal portions three times a day you will stay slim; if you eat three gargantuan portions, whether in three sittings or spread throughout the day as you nibble, graze, and gorge, then you will get fat. To eat less you need to reduce your eating capacity, and keep it that way.

Ninety percent of my clients find to their delight that they cannot eat as much as they used to before learning to eat orgasmically. The size of their stomachs has literally shrunk through eating less. The same is not necessarily true of slim dieters. Radiology has established that the stomach size of overweight people can be smaller than that of slim people. This is because, although they eat a lot overall, many fatties nibble, snack, eat, or overeat regularly throughout the day, while obsessive dieters, after dieting or starving all day, go on a big binge, extending their stomachs in the process.

Maintaining a reduced eating capacity plays an important part in maintaining your shape, and the only way to do this is by giving your stomach muscles a chance to contract when you have overdone it. The control rhythm, below, which can be used both to lose your last seven pounds and to stay in shape, alternates days of relaxed eating with control days, helping you to keep those stomach muscles in training.

Keep in Rhythm and You Will Keep in Shape

Once you have lost weight and are in shape (with a BMI some-where in between 19 and 25, depending on your body type – *see page 45*), you can return to eating the amount of three normal platefuls daily, and stop counting foods. If you have lost weight through eating orgasmically for a month or more, you should now have adapted the basic rhythm to suit your-self or tuned into your own completely individual rhythm. You can maintain this rhythm indefinitely, increasing the amount you eat to the equivalent of three platefuls, until or unless changes in your lifestyle require you to establish a different rhythm. All you need to do is to compensate by eating within the inner rim whenever you overdo it.

If you are not yet confident of maintaining your shape, or worried that once you return to eating a normal amount you will not be able to stop, then go onto the control rhythm.

The Control Rhythm

Use this rhythm to lose your last seven pounds slowly—at the rate of half to one pound a week, or to stay in shape and reduce your eating capacity. The last seven pounds is often the most difficult to lose, and if you lose more than a pound a week you are likely to regain it. Also, as you approach your ideal shape, your weight may begin to fluctuate by a few pounds. Few people maintain the exact same weight day in, day out. Hormones and daily variations in eating patterns account for a variation of about two pounds more or less in most people, so if the weight at which you look and feel your best is 126 lb, then your weight will probably fluctuate between 124 and 128 pounds. In some women the premenstrual gain will be greater.

You can also use the control rhythm as your introduction to eating orgasmically, if you are at your correct weight or have only seven pounds to lose. However, if you have ever been a dieter then be sure to practice the three mental exercises, and if you run into any difficulties—you feel uncomfortable with your rhythm or you are not losing weight—then try the basic rhythm (*see page 113*) or read the advice on the first few weeks of eating orgasmically which follows it.

The control rhythm allows you to alternate three days of *controlled* eating, eating less than you normally would, with two days of *normal* eating (the equivalent of three normal rims a day, or nine foods) and two days of *social* eating, eating orgasmically whenever you wish so long as you compensate afterwards.

Control Days
If you still have a few pounds to lose: Eat the equivalent of two normal rims a day, or six foods on your control days.

If you want to maintain your weight: You may find you can increase the amount you eat on control days by one inner rim, or one or two foods. Alternatively you can reduce the number of control days in the week to two rather than three.

Just as you lose weight by eating a little less than your body needs to satisfy its energy requirements, you stay slim by matching your food intake to your energy output (*see Metabolism, page 62*). This may sound like a very delicate balancing act, but once your body is back in equilibrium and your hunger-satiety mechanism reactivated by allowing yourself to become hungry in between meals, your body will find this balance for you naturally by telling you when to eat and when to stop (*see page 69*). If you still feel unsure quite how much you can eat either to slim or to stay slim, you can find out very quickly through trial and error, and a daily check with the scales (*see Weighing Yourself, page 167*).

To ensure that your body does not rebel by demanding more food, you should not plan for more than two consecutive control days. If, for example, you work during the week and socialize mainly at weekends, then Monday and Tuesday are good days to practice controlled eating, allowing your stomach to contract again after any excesses at the weekend. On Wednesday and Thursday you can return to eating normally, then on Friday back again to controlled eating so that your stomach has a day in which to contract again before you indulge in unrestrained eating again at the weekend. By exercising your stomach muscles, tightening them on control days and relaxing them at other times, your overall eating and drinking capacity will decrease, so that even when you eat orgasmically on noncontrol days you will find that you eat less than you would have done previously.

If you have highly active taste buds, or if your taste buds are overstimulated after eating orgasmically, follow the quiet rhythm (*see page 126*) on your control days, eating bland fat-free foods, and foods of the same or a similar type.

Example of the control rhythm

	Control	Control	Normal
	Monday	**Tuesday**	**Wednesday**
Up	6.30 – 7 A.M.	6.30 – 7 A.M.	6.30 – 7 A.M.
Bed	10 – 11 A.M.	10 – 11 A.M.	10 – 11 A.M.
Start work	8.30 – 9 A.M.	8.30 – 9 A.M.	8.30 – 9 A.M.
Finish work	5 – 5.30 P.M.	5 – 5.30 P.M.	5 – 5.30 P.M.
	10 A.M. bran, a little milk (●●)	**10 A.M.** bowl of cereal, a little milk (●●)	**7 A.M.** banana (●)
	2 P.M. granola bar (●●)	**2 P.M.** soup, or pasta with sauce (●●)	**12 – 1 P.M.** ham sandwich, chocolate bar (●●●●)
	6 – 7 P.M. baked potato and tuna salad (●●)	**6 – 7 P.M.** pasta with tomato sauce (●●)	**5 – 6 P.M.** chicken, 1 potato, 1 vegetable (●●●●)
Drinks	7 drinks daily + 2 – 3 glasses of water	7 drinks daily + 2 – 3 glasses of water	7 drinks daily + 2 – 3 glasses of water

Normal Thursday	Control Friday	Happy Saturday	Happy Sunday
6.30 – 7 A.M.	6.30 – 7 A.M.	9 – 10 A.M.	9 – 10 A.M.
10 – 11 A.M.	10 – 11 A.M.	midnight – 1 A.M.	midnight
8.30 – 9 A.M.	8.30 – 9 A.M.		
5 – 5.30 P.M.	5 – 5.30 P.M.		
7 A.M. orange	**10 A.M.** cereal, a little milk	**9 A.M.** croissant	
12 – 1 P.M. beef taco chocolate bar	**2 P.M.** pasta with sauce	**1 – 2 P.M.** soup	**1 – 2 P.M.** traditional Sunday lunch, ice cream sundae
5 – 6 P.M. tuna casserole, 1 vegetable banana	**6 – 7 P.M.** fish with tartare sauce, 1 vegetable	**7 – 8 P.M.** meal out: Indian chicken curry	**7 – 8 P.M.** banana
7 drinks daily + 2 – 3 glasses of water	7 drinks daily + 2 – 3 glasses of water	7 drinks daily + 2 – 3 glasses of water	7 drinks daily + 2 – 3 glasses of water

165

Normal Days

On your two days weekly of eating normally allow yourself the amount of three normal rims daily, compensating when you overdo it.

Social Eating and Orgasmic Days

When you eat orgasmically you should forget rims and stop counting foods. Just eat to your heart's content and enjoy every mouthful. Pay back with an inner rim when convenient!

By alternating in this way, your eating and drinking rhythm will consist of normal eating days, control eating days, and eating orgasmically, but not dieting and binges!

Finding Your Own Rhythm

Just as most slimmers find their own way to adapt the basic rhythm, now that you are in shape—or nearly so—you will discover how easy it is to adapt the control rhythm to suit your lifestyle. Your control days can be whenever convenient, changing every week to suit your particular schedule for the week.

Although in the early stages, especially for those of us with very lively taste buds, establishing your own version of the control rhythm is important, once you have internalized the art of eating and the art of compensation, you will no longer need to plan or impose a rhythm. Your own rhythm will naturally emerge, as you automatically pay back after overeating. Many of my former patients have gourmet tastes, needing quality rather than quantity to peak. They maintain their weight without control days, simply eating approximately the same amount of food every day, and compensating if they overdo it. They have absorbed and digested the art of eating so completely that it has become second nature. Once you have reached your perfect shape, eating orgasmically makes staying in shape very simple. If you gain a few pounds, say on vacation or over the winter holiday—though if you follow the vacation and winter holiday rhythms (below) you can avoid that too!—then all you need to do is pay back a little more for a few days or weeks.

> *Remember: The Name of the Game is*
> *Quantity…Quantity…Quantity!*

A balanced diet with good-quality food will help keep you fit, but it is only by reducing the quantity of what you eat that you will lose weight and stay in shape.

Weighing Yourself

If you have overcome your obsession with dieting and no longer feel guilty when you eat several eclairs on the trot, then you can weigh yourself daily if you wish, as this will give you an insight into your current eating capacity and let you know in which direction, if any, your weight is moving in. After a happy eating and drinking weekend you will naturally weigh more, then less again on a Friday as you regain control during the week. Make allowances for hormonal ups and downs as well as emotional ups and downs (postpone stepping on the scales for a few days if you know it will only depress you!), and the natural fluctuations in weight which are experienced by most people regardless.

Rhythms of Life

Just as we experience a rhythm to our lives on a daily or weekly basis, from which emerges our natural eating rhythm at any given time, so we experience a cyclical rhythm of life, marked by seasons, vacations, and festivals, and punctuated by periods of employment, unemployment, studying, traveling, single living, cohabitation, and family life, and so on. Life events and changes such as a new job or getting married may mean that you need to adapt or entirely rethink your eating rhythm, but temporary conditions just call for temporary rhythms.

Keeping in shape when your normal rhythm and routine goes out the window—especially during the annual food extravaganzas of the holiday season—can be a challenge! And if the turkey and pumpkin pies of Thanksgiving do not overly tempt you, sophisticated foodies with a passion for the exotic may find their desire to sample new and different tastes can easily lead to overindulgence and overexpansion when traveling and vacationing abroad. But forewarned is forearmed. You may of course decide to indulge to the hilt and take care of the pounds later—the damage done in a week or two is normally repaired in a week or two. But by eating artfully I have found that you really can have your cake and eat it! If you compensate, you can indulge yourself *every day* without putting on any weight. Below are examples of rhythms you can use to enjoy the fun and the food of vacations and holiday feasting while you stay in shape.

The Vacation Rhythm

Are you ready to bare your all—or nearly all—on the beach, soaking up the sun in Florida or the Caribbean? Perhaps you are off on a gastronomic tour of France, your itinerary revolving around alfresco restaurants and busy brasseries, or exploring the ancient monuments and cities of classical Greece, Rome, or Petra. Wherever you are going, and whatever you are doing, vacations are times for resting, relaxing, sightseeing, exploring, and enjoying yourself—not for worry-ing about your weight.

You want to look your best on vacation and still eat orgas-mically, so use the basic rhythm to lose weight before you go if you need to, but aim to maintain, not lose, weight while you are away. When you take a break, your whole rhythm of life—eating, drinking, and sleeping, changes—but even on holiday your body likes to maintain an eating and drinking rhythm, and the old rules still apply. Do not forget to compensate with the inner rim.

If you have adventurous taste buds, you will want to try the native cuisine wherever you stay, tasting all the local spe-cialities. This will stimulate active taste buds and you may find that to avoid putting on weight your best bet is to avoid or eat a light, bland breakfast (unless, of course, breakfast also pre-sents new and unusual foods), followed by either a light lunch and a large evening meal, or a heavy lunch and just a taste of dinner. For years I came back from vacation wearing floppy shirts and loosened belts, having continuously overeaten for a week or two, and would go into hiding for a few days before venturing out to meet my friends. Since then I have learned how to stick to the above routine.

As a guide to whether or not you are keeping in shape, take with you a pair of tight-fitting nonstretch pants and try them on every day or two. When you experience difficulty in doing them up, return to the inner rim of your plate that day. *(See page 188.)*

Deanna's Chocolate Holiday Rhythm

I would not like to pretend that a staple diet of chocolate is the most healthy, but exceptional times require exceptional measures. And, so far as chocoholics like me are concerned,

Valentine's Day and Easter are exceptional times, times for eating chocolate in exceptionally large quantities.

Unless you suffer from a condition such as diabetes or hypoglycemia, making a meal of chocolate for a few days will not do you any harm, so long as you eat at least one balanced meal during the day. And after a few days, you will probably be so satiated with chocolate that your chocolate-eating capacity will wain. *(see page 190.)*

The Winter Holiday Rhythm

The party season stretches out from the middle of December, when the first holiday parties begin, to well into the New Year. If you are a serious partygoer, this is the time of year when you really let your hair down and enjoy yourself to the hilt, nibbling and feasting orgasmically nearly every day, not to mention drinking a lot more than usual! So, if you want to have a ball yet still fit into your party frocks and glad rags by the time the season is drawing to a close, you will need to eat artfully, paying back more than usual in between your orgasmic food experiences. Even if you are enjoying a quietish holiday time and New Year with family or friends, this is still the time of good cheer, when you eat traditional foods and plenty of them, and toast the coming of holidays and the beginning of a new year with a drink or two. You, too, can enjoy orgasmic food yet keep in shape if you practice the art of eating and compensation.

Holiday parties and New Year's Eve are special occasions for highly orgasmic and indulgent eating, but if you do not want to completely let rip at every opportunity afforded throughout the long holiday period, then keep control at parties where lots of nibbles are on offer, or where a buffet is served, by limiting the number of different foods you eat.

The more variety you allow yourself, the more you will eat, especially if you have foodaholic tendencies! And watch what you drink, too. If your glass is being constantly topped up, think about putting it down to one side or alternating between mineral water and wine. The added bonus is that you will certainly feel better for it the next day!

If you are partying at night, eating and drinking until late, then avoid breakfast and keep to bland foods by day to give your overstimulated taste buds a chance to recover, and practice the three mental exercises whenever you feel you are getting out of control! By using the rhythm on page 192, or your own variation of it, you may not lose weight but you will keep in shape.

Eat orgasmically throughout the holiday and the New Year, reaching your orgasmic climax to the seasonal festivities with a New Year's feast to celebrate the dawning of a new year —and the dawning of a lifetime of eating for pleasure while you slim and stay slim. *(See page 192.)*

* * *

EATING ORGASMICALLY WILL NOT FAIL YOU.
EAT ORGASMICALLY ... AND ENJOY IT!

Appendix

Example of the bingeing rhythm

	Monday	Tuesday	Wednesday
Up	7 A.M.	7 A.M.	7 A.M.
Bed	11 P.M.	11 P.M.	11 P.M.
Start work	9 A.M.	9 A.M.	9 A.M.
Finish work	5 P.M.	5 P.M.	5 P.M.
Midday		giant cheese biscuit	giant cheese biscuit
4 P.M.	8 oz cheese, bread roll	6 oz cheese, bread roll	4 oz cheese, bread roll
6 – 9 P.M.	2 lb cheese, small salad	1 lb cheese, 2 bread rolls	8 oz cheese, 1 large apple

Thursday	Friday	Saturday	Sunday
7 A.M.	7 A.M.	7 A.M.	7 A.M.
11 P.M.	11 P.M.	11 P.M.	11 P.M.
9 A.M.	9 A.M.		
5 P.M.	5 P.M.		
giant cheese biscuit	giant cheese biscuit	giant cheese biscuit	Traditionally Sunday lunch
4 oz cheese, bread roll	4 oz cheese, bread roll		
4 oz cheese, 1 bread roll, 1 apple	fish in cheese sauce, 1 large baked potato	out for a Chinese meal	2 oz cheese, 1 apple

Example of a shift worker's rhythm

	Monday	Tuesday	Wednesday
Up	7 A.M.	7 A.M.	7 A.M.
Bed	1 A.M.	1 A.M.	1 A.M.
Start work	1st job: 8 A.M. 2nd job: 7 P.M.	1st job: 8 A.M. 2nd job: 7 P.M.	1st job: 8 A.M. 2nd job: 7 P.M.
Finish work	1st job: 1 P.M. 2nd job: midnight	1st job: 1 P.M. 2nd job: midnight	1st job: 1 P.M. 2nd job: midnight
9 A.M.	toasted giant corn muffin, a little margarine	raspberry bar cookie	Chocolate chip muffin
1 P.M.	pasta with sauce	beef taco	pasta with sauce
6 P.M.	Mexican take-out	pasta salad	Mexican take-out
12.30 A.M.	soup	soup	roll
Drinks	7 drinks plus 2 – 3 glasses of water	7 drinks plus 2 – 3 glasses of water	7 drinks plus 2 – 3 glasses of water

Thursday	Friday	Saturday	Sunday
7 A.M.	7 A.M.	10 A.M.	10 A.M.
1 A.M.	1 A.M.	10 P.M.	10 P.M.
1st job: 8 A.M. 2nd job: 7 P.M.	1st job: 8 A.M. 2nd job: 7 P.M.		
1st job: 1 P.M. 2nd job: midnight	1st job: 1 P.M. 2nd job: midnight		
pastry	banana	pay back	pay back
pasta with sauce	small salad, chicken	fish and fries, peas, ice cream	Sunday Brunch; fruit
pizza, salad	Chinese take-out	pay back	pay back
soup	roll		
7 drinks plus 2 – 3 glasses of water	7 drinks plus 2 – 3 glasses of water	7 drinks plus 2 – 3 glasses of water	7 drinks plus 2 – 3 glasses of water

Example of a barperson's rhythm

	Monday	Tuesday	Wednesday
Up	8.00 A.M.	8.00 A.M.	8.00 A.M.
Bed	1.30 A.M.	1.30 A.M.	1.30 A.M.
Work	9 A.M. – 3 P.M. 6 P.M. – midnight	day off	day off
8.30 A.M.	coffee	coffee	coffee
12.30 A.M.	burger and french fries banana	chicken pot pie	steak, baked potato

| **6 p.m.** | 4 oz fish with tartare
sauce, 1 serving
vegetables | 4 oz fish in
sauce, 1 serving
vegetables,
1 potato | ham sandwich |

| **Midnight** | soup | soup | apple |

| **Drinks** | 7 drinks daily | 7 drinks daily | 7 drinks daily |

Thursday	Friday	Saturday	Sunday
8.00 A.M.	8.00 A.M.	8.00 A.M.	8.00 A.M.
1.30 A.M.	1.30 A.M.	1.30 A.M.	12.30 A.M.
9 A.M. – 3 P.M. 6 P.M. – midnight	9 A.M. – 3 P.M. 6 P.M. – midnight	9 A.M. – 3 P.M. 6 P.M. – midnight	9 A.M. – 3 P.M. 6 P.M. – midnight
coffee	coffee	coffee	coffee
burger and french fries, banana	beef burrito	chicken salad	Sunday pot roast, with 1 potato, 1 vegetable, 1 dinner roll
(3)	(2)	(3)	(shaded)
steak pie, 1 serving vegetables, gravy	4 oz fish with tartare sauce, baked potato	roast beef, baked potato, gravy	1 orange
(3)	(3)	(3)	(1)
soup	banana	banana	soup
(1)	(1)	(1)	(1)
7 drinks daily	7 drinks daily	7 drinks daily	7 drinks daily

179

Example of a high flier's rhythm

	Monday	Tuesday	Wednesday
Up	6 A.M.	6 A.M.	6 A.M.
Bed	11 P.M.	midnight	midnight – 1 A.M.
Start work	7 A.M.	7 A.M.	7 A.M.
Finish work	7 P.M. or later	7 P.M. or later	7.30 P.M.
9 A.M.	banana	banana	small bowl of bran, a little milk
1 P.M.	cold cut sandwich	business lunch: 3 courses, wine	orange
8 P.M.	fish with tartare sauce, 2 spoons vegetables, no alcohol	pay back: clear soup = 1 drink	business dinner: 3 course meal, wine
Drinks	7 drinks daily	7 drinks daily	7 drinks daily

Thursday	Friday	Saturday	Sunday
6 A.M.	6 A.M.	9 A.M.	10 A.M.
midnight – 1 A.M.	midnight	midnight – 1 A.M.	midnight
7 A.M.	7 A.M.		
7.30 P.M.	10 P.M. or later		
pay back	too full	bowl of cereal, a little milk	pay back
		●●	
banana, a little bran, milk	lunch out: 3 courses, wine	baked salmon	Sunday lunch: roast beef, potatoes, dinner rolls, vegetables
⦂●	◯(grey)	●●	◯(grey)
meal out, 3 courses, wine	orange	baked potato, salad, no alcohol	1 muffin, margarine, no alcohol
◯(grey)	●	●●	●
7 drinks daily	7 drinks daily	7 drinks daily	7 drinks daily

181

Example of a five-year-old's rhythm to stay slim, taking

	Monday	Tuesday	Wednesday
Up	7 A.M.	7 A.M.	7 A.M.
Bed	8 P.M. – 8.30 P.M.	8 P.M. – 8.30 P.M.	8 P.M. – 8.30 P.M.
Start school	9 A.M.	9 A.M.	9 A.M.
Finish school	3.30 P.M.	3.30 P.M.	3.30 P.M.
8 A.M.	cereal, milk	cereal, milk	cereal, milk
10.30 A.M.	milk or juice, cookies	milk or juice, cookies	milk or juice, cookies
12.30 – 1 P.M.	pasta, salad, low-fat yogurt	egg salad sandwich, apple	cold cuts, cherry tomatoes, cucumber, low-fat yogurt
3.30 – 4 P.M.	apple or chips	apple or chips	apple or chips
6.30 – 7.30 P.M.	chicken nuggets, fries, raw vegetables, e.g. carrots, cucumber	sausages, beans, raw vegetables	baked potato, cheese, candy
Drinks	7 drinks daily	7 drinks daily	7 drinks daily

NB Often much of the food is left half eaten.

packed lunch to school

Thursday	Friday	Saturday	Sunday
7 A.M.	7 A.M.	7.30 A.M.	7.30 A.M.
8 P.M. – 8.30 P.M.	8 P.M. – 8.30 P.M.	9.00 P.M.	7.30 – 8.30 P.M.
9 A.M.	9 A.M.		
3.30 P.M.	3.30 P.M.		
toast, peanut butter	chocolate pastry	toast, peanut butter	cereal, milk
milk or juice, cookies	milk or juice, cookies	apple	apple
peanut butter sandwiches, low-fat yogurt	pasta, raw vegetables, piece of cheese	salmon, mashed potato, ice cream	olives, fish sticks, french fries
apple or chips	apple or chips	packet of candy	popcorn
fish sticks, french fries, peas or beans	chicken dinosaurs, alphabet potatoes, green beans	pasta, salad banana and custard	scrambled egg and toast
7 drinks daily	7 drinks daily	7 drinks daily	7 drinks daily

Deanna's chocolate rhythm

	Monday	Tuesday	Wednesday
Up	7.30 A.M.	7.30 A.M.	7.30 A.M.
Bed	11 P.M.	11 P.M.	11 P.M.
Start work	9.30 A.M.	9.30 A.M.	9.30 A.M.
Finish work	5.30 P.M.	5.30 P.M.	5.30 P.M.
9 – 10 A.M.	banana	banana	banana
1 P.M.	2 large Snicker bars	2 large Snicker bars	2 large Snicker bars
6 – 7 P.M.	salmon in sauce, peas and carrots	lemon sole in cheese sauce, potatoes, cake	chicken Kiev, broccoli
Drinks	7 drinks daily	7 drinks daily	7 drinks daily

Thursday	Friday	Saturday	Sunday
7.30 A.M.	7.30 A.M.	7.30 A.M.	7.30 A.M.
11 P.M.	11 P.M.	midnight	11 – midnight
9.30 A.M.	9.30 A.M.		
5.30 P.M.	5.30 P.M.		
apple	apple		
2 large Snicker bars	2 large Snicker bars	1 giant bar of chocolate	pot roast, glazed carrots, mustard, mashed potatoes, broccoli with almonds, pecan pie
Stir-fry, rice, salad	barbecued salmon, fried rice with peppers	out to dinner, 4 courses	
7 drinks daily	7 drinks daily	7 drinks daily	7 drinks daily

185

Example of an exercise rhythm

	Monday	Tuesday	Wednesday
Up	6.30 – 7 A.M.	6.30 – 7 A.M.	6.30 – 7 A.M.
Bed	10 – 11 P.M.	10 – 11 P.M.	10 – 11 P.M.
Start work	9 – 9.30 A.M.	9 – 9.30 A.M.	9 – 9.30 A.M.
Finish work	5 – 5.30 P.M.	5 – 5.30 P.M.	5 – 5.30 P.M.
8 – 9 A.M.	2 serving spoons bran, a little milk	apple	2 serving spoons bran, a little milk
12 – 1 P.M.	burger and fries	noodle casserole	pasta casserole
5 P.M.	banana	muffin	banana
6 – 7 P.M.	aerobic exercise in gym	aerobic exercise in gym	aerobic exercise in gym
7 – 8 P.M.	salmon with hollandaise sauce, 1 vegetable	beans on toast	large baked potato with tuna
Drinks	7 drinks + daily	7 drinks + daily	7 drinks + daily

Thursday	Friday	Saturday	Sunday
6.30 – 7 A.M.	6.30 – 7 A.M.	9 – 10 A.M.	9 – 10 A.M.
10 – 11 P.M.	10 – 11 P.M.	midnight – 1 A.M.	midnight
9 – 9.30 A.M.	9 – 9.30 A.M.		
5 – 5.30 P.M.	5 – 5.30 P.M.		
banana			
burger and fries	chocolate chip muffin	soup, roll	traditional Sunday pot roast
granola bar	pear	peach	
aerobic exercise in gym	aerobic exercise in gym	aerobic exercise in gym	
shrimp salad	Italian meal out	Chinese/Mexican meal out	pear
7 drinks + daily	7 drinks + daily	7 drinks + daily	7 drinks + daily

Example of a vacation rhythm

	Monday	Tuesday	Wednesday
Up	9 A.M.	9 A.M.	9 A.M.
Bed	midnight – 1 A.M.	midnight – 1 A.M.	midnight – 1 A.M.
9.30 A.M.	pot of coffee, almond croissant	pot of coffee, almond croissant	pot of coffee, almond croissant
1 P.M.	small salad	open-faced sandwich	peach
4 P.M.	iced tea, chocolate gateau	iced tea, ice-cream cake	peach
7.30 – 8.30 P.M.	scallop and fennel salad; crispy roast duck breasts with potato purée; pears in coffee syrup; coffee, cookies	curried tartlet; lamb fillet, spinach timbale; stuffed figs in ginger sauce	artichoke hearts in cream; lobster with dill dressing; carrot cake with icing
Drinks	7 drinks daily	7 drinks daily	7 drinks daily

Thursday	Friday	Saturday	Sunday
9 A.M.	9 A.M.	9 – 10 A.M.	9 – 10 A.M.
midnight – 1 A.M.	midnight – 1 A.M.	midnight – 1 A.M.	midnight – 1 A.M.
pot of coffee, almond croissant	pot of coffee, almond croissant	pot of coffee, almond croissant	pot of coffee, almond croissant
peach			watercress, pasta with mussels
	tea, pecan pie		
lobster ravioli; pan fried cod, potatoes, spinach; fruit cocktail	fillet of trout and chervil cream sauce; stuffed guinea fowl, asparagus	vegetable gratin; duck and watercress pâté; chocolate hazelnut soufflé; coffee, cookies	smoked salmon and crab roll; roast pigeon with savoury mousse; cinnamon crumb cake
7 drinks daily	7 drinks daily	7 drinks daily	7 drinks daily

Deanna's chocolate holiday rhythm
(for maintaining rather than losing weight)

	Monday	Tuesday	Wednesday
Up	9 A.M.	9 A.M.	9 A.M.
Bed	midnight	midnight	10.30 P.M.
Start work		8 A.M.	8 A.M.
Finish work		5 P.M.	5 P.M.
10 A.M.	orange (● 1)	cereal, a little milk (●● 2)	cereal, a little milk (●● 2)
1 P.M.	whole Easter egg (●●● 3)	steak and potatoes, peas, red wine sauce (●●● 3)	noodle casserole (●● 2)
4 P.M.		tea, cookies (● 1)	tea, 2 cookies (●● 2)
8 P.M.	smoked salmon, small salad (●● 2)	honey roast ham, 1 vegetable, 1 potato (●●● 3)	1 serving lamb stew, 2 serving spoons petit pois (●●● 3)
Drinks	7 drinks daily	7 drinks daily	7 drinks daily

Thursday	Friday	Saturday	Sunday
9 A.M.	9 A.M.	9 A.M.	9 A.M.
10.30 P.M.	midnight	midnight	midnight
8 A.M.			
5 P.M.			
cereal, a little milk	cereal, a little milk	cereal, a little milk	brunch: dried fruit compôte in wine; bacon, egg,
fried rice	noodle casserole	cup of clear soup, roll	sausage, cheese grits, pancakes, toast and honey
tea, 2 cookies	banana	cookies	
grilled chicken, 3 slices of peppers	fish with tartare sauce, 1 potato	Mexican meal, dessert	whole Easter bunny and chocolates
7 drinks daily	7 drinks daily	7 drinks daily	7 drinks daily

Example of a holiday rhythm

	Christmas Day	Day after Christmas	Thursday
Up	9 A.M.	9 A.M.	9 A.M.
Bed	1 A.M.	1 A.M.	1 A.M.
9.30 A.M.	coffee	coffee	coffee
1 – 2 P.M.	nibbles of nuts, dried fruits, chocolates	fruit, cheese	cold roast beef, or turkey, rolls
4 – 5 P.M.	Christmas cookies, champagne	Christmas cookies, champagne	chocolates, cocktails
7 – 10 P.M.	traditional Christmas dinner, wine	"left-overs" buffet, wine	nibbles of fruit and nuts

Friday	Saturday	Sunday	New Year's Eve
9 A.M.	9 A.M.	9 A.M.	9 A.M.
1 A.M.	1 A.M.	1 A.M.	2 A.M.
coffee	coffee	coffee	coffee
beef stew	bowl of dried fruit compôte in kirsch	all day brunch party	smoked salmon sandwich
coffee and chocolates			
plateful of fruit	turkey sandwich, salad		roast pork, peas, potatoes, pecan pie, whipped cream, wine, champagne

Index

full–hungry rhythm 69, 71, 90–1

W

waiting 83, 91–3, 130
water retention 66–7, 68
weighing yourself 106, 120,
    145, 167
  ideal weight 51–5
  target weight 51
weight loss 112–42
  plateaux 110–11
  stopped 140–1

willpower, in mental exercises
    82, 85–7
Winter Holiday rhythm 167,
    168, 170–1, 192–3
working hours, irregular,
    rhythms for 144, 145–9

Y

yoyo dieting 3–4, 6–7, 35, 36,
    38, 41